I0160547

THE RELATIONS OF LEARNING

THE
RELATIONS OF
LEARNING

A SERIES OF ADDRESSES ON UNIVERSITY EDUCATION
IN A CHANGING WORLD

WILLIAM BENNETT BIZZELL

NORMAN
UNIVERSITY OF OKLAHOMA PRESS
MCMXXXIV

The Relations of Learning, by William Bennett Bizzell

Copyright 1934 by the University of Oklahoma Press

SET UP AND PRINTED AT NORMAN, OKLAHOMA, U.S.A., BY THE UNIVERSITY OF
OKLAHOMA PRESS, PUBLISHING DIVISION OF THE UNIVERSITY
FIRST EDITION NOVEMBER 15, 1934

UXORI DILECTISSIMÆ

APOLOGIA

I T H A S long been a custom at the University of Oklahoma for the president to deliver an address to a general convocation at the opening of each scholastic year. This book is composed, in the main, of the addresses delivered on these occasions during the past ten years. It has seemed desirable to include in the volume, in addition to these convocational papers, the author's inaugural address delivered on February 5, 1926; the address at Iowa State College, Ames, on May 24, 1934; and an article that appeared in the March (1934) number of *The University of Chicago Magazine*. While the inaugural address was delivered under entirely different circumstances from the convocational addresses and the article in *The University of Chicago Magazine* differs in form from the other material, both bear upon the general subject of this volume.

The inaugural address is placed first, for it seems to serve in a general way as an introduction to the subsequent discussions. The article on "The Changing State University" and the address on "The Quality of Learning" are made the concluding chapters, as they attempt to give a forward look to the general scheme of higher education, particularly higher education as fostered by our state universities.

The author is fully aware that the philosophy of learning is not subject to temporal limitations, but the educational process that fosters learning is influenced by the historical perspective. Educational thought and opportunity have experienced profound transformations during the past few years. It is hoped, therefore, that a certain timeliness may

[vii]

appear in these discussions, for a sincere effort has been made to relate the various aspects of learning to the changing social, political, economic, and educational situation.

The publication of this volume gives the author an opportunity to acknowledge his great appreciation to his associates on the several faculties and to the hundreds of students who have listened to these discussions. It is not assumed, of course, that they have been equally interesting to all those who have been present on these several occasions. It is freely admitted that the subject matter would not be equally interesting to students at the various levels of learning. The motive behind the preparation of these addresses has been the desire to stimulate an interest in scholarship and to impress students with the primary purpose of college life.

The author wishes, also, to express his appreciation to Mr. Joseph A. Brandt, the scholarly editor of the University of Oklahoma Press, for the encouragement that has caused these papers to be prepared for publication and for the attractive typography and format in which they appear. The author cannot express in words his genuine appreciation for the assistance that has been rendered by Mr. Brandt in connection with the publication of this book.

These addresses are presented in this form with the hope that they may make an appeal to a larger public. Should they serve in any way to stimulate academic idealism and to promote interest in scholarship, the author will be gratified and their publication in this form justified.

WILLIAM BENNETT BIZZELL

University of Oklahoma,
Norman, Oklahoma.
October 31, 1934.

CONTENTS

THE RELATIONS OF LEARNING

THE EDUCATIONAL OBLIGATIONS OF

A STATE UNIVERSITY[1]

CHAPTER ONE

A CHANGE of administration in an important educational institution always creates problems and results in anxiety and uncertainty. It usually means some lost motion and more or less disorganization. There is no standard type of college or university administrator. Institutions differ just as men differ. This means that every time there is a change of administration it is necessary for the official to learn to work with the several faculties and they must learn to work with him. A college organization is composed of many types of personalities. As a rule the university president is also a distinct type of personality. The general public has no conception of how many adjustments need to be made in a transition of this kind.

I am not unmindful of the great responsibility that devolves upon a governing board in selecting a president for an educational institution. The public expects a governing board to maintain an efficient organization in the institution whose affairs it directs. Much depends, therefore, upon the qualities of the man who is selected for the task of directing a complex organization like the University of Oklahoma. I have never known exactly why the Board of Regents invited me to accept this position. I was in no sense an

1. Inaugural address delivered on February 5, 1926.

applicant for the place; and I naturally assume if I had been, I would not have received the appointment. But since the Board of Regents has called me to this service, I feel very keenly the responsibility of fulfilling their expectations.

It is only just that I publicly acknowledge my profound sense of appreciation for the spirit of co-operation I have received since I came to the university. I doubt that any man who has ever been called to a position of this kind in this country ever received a more cordial welcome or a more widespread and sincere expression of good will than has come to me. The administrative officers and the members of the several faculties, without exception, have manifested the finest spirit of co-operation. The people of Norman have given me and mine a whole-hearted welcome. The officials of the state have shown a helpful attitude. The citizenship generally has expressed in a thousand ways its desire to help me in the important task of building a greater university in this state. The Board of Regents pledged me its whole-hearted support before I came. This board knows the distinction between governmental policies and administrative practices. They never lose sight of the line of demarcation in their deliberations. This is the highest compliment I can pay our Board of Regents, for this is a rare quality in governing boards. It is quite apparent, therefore, that if I fail to measure up to the requirements of this position, I cannot place the blame on anyone but myself.

I formally accept today, in the presence of this great group of scholarly men and women, the task set before me. I enter upon my work with a profound sense of the responsibility involved in administering a great state-supported institution, and I accept the challenge implied by the invitation extended me by the Board of Regents to contribute a man's part in the supreme task of building in Oklahoma a university worthy of a great people.

I remind the visitors assembled here today that the University of Oklahoma antedates statehood. The State of Oklahoma is only eighteen years old. It is only thirty-six years since the opening of this country to settlement. The university had its origin in a legislative enactment of the Territory of Oklahoma, which was approved on December 19, 1890. The institution opened its doors in the fall of 1892. This beautiful campus and these attractive buildings are the product of only thirty-three years of planning and effort on the part of those who have guided the destinies of the university.

The University of Oklahoma has followed about the same course as the other forty-four state universities. The growth of the institution was rather slow in the early years, but in recent years it has grown with remarkable rapidity. Probably no state in the Union has made greater economic or material progress since statehood than this state has made. The educational progress of the state has kept pace with the increase in wealth and population.

The University of Oklahoma has been fortunate in its teaching force and administrative officers. There have always been strong men and conscientious women identified with the university who have set good standards of academic instruction. Throughout the history of the institution earnest and unselfish men have guided its destinies. There have only been five men who have served as president of the university. President David Ross Boyd, whose administration covered the first sixteen years of the university, laid the foundation, shaped the campus out of the boundless prairie, and created for the institution a place of respect in the academic world. President A. Grant Evans stamped the institution with fine culture and high purpose. President Stratton D. Brooks served the institution for eleven years, having directed its affairs through the critical period of the World War. He stamped his personality upon the institution for all time to come. At critical periods in the university's history, Deans Julien C. Monnet and James Shannon Buchanan have served as presidents of the institution in a highly satisfactory manner. I am not unmindful of the high standards of efficiency that my honored predecessors have set, and I feel a deep sense of humility in undertaking to perform the duties that they performed so well.

If the University of Oklahoma is to fulfill its purpose and justify the faith that the people have imposed in it, those of us responsible for directing its affairs must clearly conceive the objectives of the institution. Higher education has suffered in popular esteem because its purposes have not been well defined. The inevitable result has been failure to co-ordinate our efforts and to utilize our forces to the best advantage.

What are the objectives of education? What are we trying to accomplish for society through our complex educational organization? John Milton undertook to answer these questions as far back as 1644 in his *Tractate* as follows: "I hold, therefore, that a complete and generous education is that which fits a man to perform justly, skilfully, and magnanimously all the offices, both public and private, of peace and war." Another answer comes to us in the preamble to the Ordinance of 1787 providing for the organization of the Northwest Territory. "Religion, morality, and knowledge being necessary to good government and happiness of mankind, schools and the means of education shall forever be encouraged." More recently Davidson, in his *History of Education* has declared that "the aim of education is world building—the construction of such a world as shall furnish the man with motives to live an enlightened, kindly, helpful, and noble social life of continuous progress." Within the limits of these generalizations we can safely formulate our program of education:

1. The development of a more versatile and more conscientious citizenship.

2. The attainment of a more stable and a more satisfying social life.

3. A human product better fortified against human ills and physical deterioration.

4. A widespread dissemination of a knowledge of rational living.

5. Insuring to society a surplus of material goods and social advantages.

Our problem arises, however, when we attempt to particularize. The subject matter and methods of instruction required to accomplish these comprehensive objectives involve us in endless difficulty and sometimes profitless experimentation. But the more clearly we define our enthusiasm and the more definitely we conceive our aims, the more likely we are to obtain satisfying results.

Every university worthy of the name attempts to accomplish its objectives by instruction and research. Teaching is the method of disseminating knowledge already acquired. Research is the "systematic investigation of phenomena by experimental methods to discover facts or co-ordinate them into laws." I would not undertake to appraise the relative emphasis that should be placed upon these two activities in a university. But it goes without saying that both must occupy a place of great importance in every university worthy of the name. It is the peculiar function of the college to impart knowledge. Some types of colleges do more or less research, but it is the important task of the university to supplement classroom instruction and laboratory practice by both theoretical and practical investigations of many kinds.

Great progress has been made in the improvement of teaching methods in recent years. But the enormous increase in the number of students in our colleges and universities since the World War has created some rather baffling problems. The percentage of high school graduates who enter institutions of higher learning has steadily increased. The mere fact that this large number of students has decided to enter college does not mean that all of them have developed an intellectual interest or are entering college for the definite purpose of acquiring a college education. Educational administrators have not found an accurate method of differentiating between the intellectual sheep and the parasitic goats. The public has become somewhat skeptical over our failure to conserve intellectual effort and safeguard financial resources while dealing with this unassimilated mass of students. But I think we can give the public some assurance that we are reaching toward a solution by requiring more exacting entrance requirements, establishing honors courses, and adopting methods of eliminating those who fail to meet the more definite standards of instruction.

The increase in student enrolment has made it necessary to extend greatly the faculty personnel. The supply of teachers well qualified to give instruction has not been equal to the demand. The rapid differentiation in the field of knowledge has made it increasingly necessary to secure teachers of highly specialized training and experience. Personality, a real spirit of learning, and consecration to the cause of education are also important qualifications of the teacher. Our human resources have not been sufficient to supply an adequate number of men and women with these high, but essential, qualifications. The result has been inevitable, therefore, that under these conditions it has been increasingly difficult to maintain academic standards.

Incidental to this general situation has been a failure to

impart knowledge with a proper perspective. The extension of knowledge in the last generation has overwhelmed us with details. Our institutions have almost lost their educational perspective. The relativity of principles and facts has been ignored. There has been an increasing tendency to teach everything to all men and to teach everything as if it were equally important. It has not been surprising that many students have lost their intellectual way in a confusion of details.

Policies of research also deserve searching analysis. *Scientific synthesis and the prevention of waste are the objectives of research.* We know that the limits of knowledge have been greatly extended as a result of investigation. But we do not know how to make the efforts of the research worker more certain of results or how to determine the aptitudes of men best adapted to research accomplishment. We do know that an increasing number of industrial enterprises have established research activities. This would imply that our educational institutions are not supplying fully the needs of industry, commerce, and transportation with the kind of knowledge that our highly complex civilization requires today.

Our educational institutions are confronted with the necessity of making a searching analysis of their actual accomplishments in the field of pure knowledge and applied science. There is no business today that is independent of science. There is no industry that is not imperiled or advanced by scientific discovery. The chemist, the physicist, and the biologist are daily extending the boundaries of knowledge to new limits; and the engineer and scientific technologist are applying this knowledge in a thousand ways to industrial and commercial enterprises. How completely are our universities supplying the knowledge that business demands to insure orderly material progress? This question we need to keep constantly before us.

Let me bring this thought before you more concretely. The mineral resources of Oklahoma constitute the basis of the state's wealth. Petroleum, coal, zinc, and lead are produced in relatively large quantities. There are more than twenty minerals of commercial importance in this state. These resources have been largely responsible for the great prosperity of the state in recent years. Fifteen counties of the state produced over 3,000,000 tons of coal, valued at approximately $11,000,000. Government surveys estimate the coal resources of the state at 75,000,000,000 tons. More than 161,000,000 barrels of petroleum, valued at $279,-000,000, were produced in one year.

Coal and petroleum are the principal resources today of heat, light, and power. These constitute, therefore, the sustaining basis of our civilization. The rapidly increasing demand for light, heat, and power has presented a problem of the greatest importance. In 1850 the consumption of coal was less than 10,000,000 tons. In 1880 the consumption had increased to nearly 75,000,000 tons. In 1920 the consumption exceeded 1,600,000,000 tons. Experts estimate that even at the present rate of consumption our supply of bituminous coal will last only 250 years and our anthracite supply will be exhausted in about 100 years. While there are other sources of fuel, there is a real problem of getting the maximum of power out of every pound of coal. There are those who believe that all power will eventually be generated by water from reservoirs and river channels. Others think oil will gradually displace coal as a source of fuel. We need to recall, however, that coal is not only a source of power, but that explosives, dyes, medicines, road material, and numerous other by-products essential to civilization come from it.

It is possible also for modern science and engineering technology to put coal on a competitive basis with oil and even with water power. Important experiments have already been made with powdered coal and recently a German scientist has liquefied coal. What these discoveries and experiments will lead to no one can definitely predict at the present time.

Oil has become one of the really essential products of the world. There is no satisfactory substitute for some of its uses today. Yet, we are told at the present rate of consumption the available underground supply will be exhausted in less than twenty years. Stuart Chase in *The Tragedy of Waste* says: "For every barrel of oil produced three barrels or more are left underground, or wasted in well operation." These are challenging facts that cannot be ignored. The people of Oklahoma certainly cannot disregard them. Petroleum is a matter of great importance to this state. Oklahoma is the second largest oil-producing state in the United States. The value of crude petroleum and refined products constitutes approximately half the annual income of the state. We need to know all about this product. Yet the chemist tells us that we know practically nothing about petroleum. Very little has actually been done in the chemistry of petroleum. The possibilities can be realized when it is recalled that the physicists and technologists are reported to have increased the gasoline production from petroleum by 3,000,000,000 gallons annually by cracking. This accomplishment alone has made the pleasure car available to almost the entire citizenship of the nation.

The possibility of exhausting the ultimate supply of oil has caused widespread speculation with reference to a substitute. The prospect of this actually happening has caused the chemist to look elsewhere for a new fuel resource. It is generally known that alcohol is a good motor fuel. The obstacle to its use has been its limited supply. But recently both grain and wood alcohol have been synthesized. The problem of the chemist is now to produce alcohol cheaply. This is not an impossible task, as we have many examples,

[9]

such as helium gas, where a synthetic process has been developed and methods of manufacturing have ultimately been discovered that have brought the price down within reasonable limits.

I have merely indicated in the briefest possible way some of the possibilities of research of peculiar interest to the people of this state. Illustrations could be added indefinitely. I understand that twelve counties possess rock asphalt of excellent quality for paving when properly treated. The state has entered upon a great program of highway construction. It is of great importance that we build our roads of permanent material at the least possible cost. The chemist and technologist need to unite their efforts to bring this about.

I am hoping that the University of Oklahoma may realize its obligations to the people of this state by directing its energies to a vast program of research that will eliminate waste and result in new methods of utilizing our agricultural and mineral resources. To this end I pledge my best efforts with the sincere hope that the university may contribute to the economic and material advancement of the state through the output from laboratories and technological departments.

It is my earnest desire to see the research and instructional program of the university adapted to the actual and potential needs of the state. In the formulation of such a program consideration needs to be given to the problems that confront all the vocational groups of our society. The university should have a contribution to make to agricultural producers, mine, manufacture, and transportation agencies. As rapidly as resources are available, an effort will be made to adjust the research and technological activities of the university to the solution of the immediate problems growing out of these enterprises.

I believe the university has a contribution to make to

[10]

the entire school system of the state. The improvement of the rural schools in Oklahoma presents a problem of great importance. Equality of educational opportunity should be the earnest desire of our people. We know that there is no such equality today. Our rural schools are not providing adequate opportunities for the children of our farm population. The University of Oklahoma proposes to co-operate in improving this situation.

We must never forget that the essential justification for education at public expense in a democracy is training for good citizenship. We have long since learned that good laws will not guarantee a stable social order. It is not sufficient for our institutions of higher learning to supply trained leadership. It is equally necessary to train our people to follow wise leadership. Society has not done enough for any man if it has not taught him how to discriminate between the demagogue and the honest political leader. The common task of all of our schools is to supply the kind of education that will improve the quality of citizenship.

I remind you in this connection that our people still regard their obligation of citizenship rather lightly. Most of us are also inclined to define citizenship in terms of suffrage. From time to time throughout our national history we have extended the privilege of suffrage to an increasing number of our population. But it seems that the effect of this process has been a steady decline in the sense of obligation on the part of our citizenship to exercise this high privilege. This tendency has reached the point where it has become an actual menace to our institutions. At every general and special election, countless thousands of our people fail to vote. It not infrequently happens that bond issues involving the expenditure of millions of dollars are determined by a small minority of the electorate. Our educational institutions have a contribution to make to this problem and certainly no state-supported institution can afford to ignore it.

There is a widespread opinion throughout the country that there has been a decline in the standards of integrity and efficiency of public officials. Officeholding must ever be regarded as a public trust. It is not sufficient that our officials be honest; they must be intelligent and well qualified for the services they are called upon to render. It requires a high order of intelligence and unusual standards of proficiency to perform the functions of public officials today. Society has become so complex that our administrative problems are not easy of solution. The consequences of inefficiency, therefore, endanger the stability of our social order. We must look to trained leadership in public office as the hope of democracy. To accept mediocrity as an incident to our form of government is to deny the justification for the form of government under which we live. I do not accept this inference. It is my belief that our educational institutions must make contributions to society in terms of qualified men and women who can render service in public office of as high quality as that engaged in directing private enterprise.

An effort has been made to set out some of the scientific, economic, political, and social problems that should concern the citizenship of this state. I wish now to direct your attention more specifically to the contribution that the university should make to the solution of these problems.

There is a real necessity for the university to increase its research facilities. A strong graduate school in the university is demanded by every consideration of public policy. A graduate school was organized as a separate department of the university in 1909. The degrees of Master of Arts and Master of Science and the professional engineering degrees have been awarded for several years. While good standards have been maintained, the relative number of graduate courses has not been large, although the number has been rapidly increasing.

The time has come when the university should extend its facilities and provide graduate students with adequate research opportunities leading to the doctor's degree. But this implies that larger laboratory and library facilities will be available to place the research work of the institution on a high plane. The university would not be justified in entering upon a comprehensive program of graduate instruction unless the sources of material for research were so extensive and our laboratory equipment so adequate as to challenge the respect of the most promising men and women in the country. But there is no reason why this state cannot provide all the facilities necessary to make the graduate school of the university one of the most desirable agencies for public good to be found in the entire country.

Medical education has received increasing attention in recent times. Great medical centers are being established in connection with many of our state universities and privately endowed institutions. An immediate problem before us is the improvement of our facilities for medical education in Oklahoma. A conditional appropriation made by the legislature is now available for this purpose, but this fund must be matched by an equal sum from some other source. It would be a calamity for us to fail to secure the necessary funds to insure the construction of this building.

It is urgently necessary to provide courses in public health subjects as soon as possible. Oklahoma is not keeping pace with other progressive states in this regard. It is not sufficient to provide the state with an adequate number of skilled physicians to minister to our ills. It is our duty to train competent sanitarians and public health officials to safeguard the health of the people and prevent as much illness as possible. I sincerely believe that a dental school should

[13]

also be established in connection with the medical school. There is no dental school in Oklahoma. Dental education is receiving widespread attention throughout the country and Oklahoma should give consideration to the needs for dental education in this state.

I remind you also that the obligations of the state university cannot be completely fulfilled by offering instruction to a few thousand resident students. Education today is not restricted to the youth of the land. The thirst for knowledge has no age restrictions. The state-supported university must satisfy the intellectual hunger of every man and woman, regardless of age or place of residence within the state. The university should lend a helping hand to everyone who earnestly desires to increase his skill and capacity for industrial service. The public has a right to turn to the university for every kind of information that will help in the solution of economic, social, and political problems.

We must, therefore, think of the state's geographical boundaries as the limits of the university campus and the people of the state should regard the buildings here in Norman merely as the reservoirs of knowledge that they may freely tap whenever they desire. It will, therefore, be my sincere purpose to encourage every form of extension teaching and provide the facilities for the dissemination of all kinds of useful knowledge for which there may be a demand on the part of the citizenship of the state.

The public is especially concerned about the character results of the educational process. What is the effect of education upon integrity and moral life? We know that not all education is equally effective in stimulating worthy motives and generous impulses. "Experience offers proof," says George Gissing, "on every hand that vigorous mental life may be but one side of personality, of which the other is moral barbarism. A man may be a fine archaeologist, yet have no sympathy with ideals. The historian, the biographer, even the poet, may be a money-market gambler, a social toady, a clamorous chauvinist, or an unscrupulous wire-puller." We have too long assumed that intellectual attainments implied the possession of character and worthy motives. A little learning is a dangerous thing if a man expects to get to heaven by degrees. We cannot justify our educational system if it fails to provide for character training.

I am convinced that we must find a better way to articulate intellectual and moral training. We must find a place in the educational process both for emphasizing moral principles and testing the character ideals of our students. Serious consideration should be given to the content of our courses with a moral objective. Our religion is highly ethical. Our institutions must see to it that religious faith is not undermined by the content of courses that we offer or the attitude of those who impart knowledge to the student.

The increasing distribution of educational opportunity is one of the most encouraging signs of the times. Education has persistently followed in the footsteps of the pioneer. Our first colleges and universities were established on the Atlantic seaboard. Until recent times our young people looked to the East and Northeast for the best educational advantages. But with the accession of new territory and the formation of new states; with the distribution of wealth and population throughout the country, educational institutions have multiplied. More than 500,000 students are now enrolled in approximately 800 institutions of higher learning. Today every section of the country is reasonably well supplied with excellent colleges and universities.

The growth of state colleges and state universities in the Middle West in recent years has been remarkable. Education will probably make its greatest advance in the next quarter of a century in those states lying west of the Mississippi River and extending to the Rocky Mountains. The actual and potential wealth, the varied economic and commercial opportunities, and the rapid increase in population throughout this vast area seem to justify this prophecy. The University of Oklahoma is strategically located in this vast territory. The agricultural and mineral resources of the state, the rapidly increasing industrial enterprises, and the virility of its population will insure adequate financial support from public and private sources to make our educational institutions equal to the best.

There is a very definite tendency today toward intellectual co-operation. Co-operation in research is receiving increasing attention. I believe the University of Oklahoma should encourage this movement. We should encourage students from other states and foreign countries to come to this institution for such professional, technical, and graduate instruction as our facilities may make attractive. Fellowships should be made available for some of our most promising students who could more profitably do part of their research work in some other institution. I sincerely hope that funds for this purpose may be provided by citizens of the state who appreciate the importance of endowing men and women of unusual ability to the end that they may be enabled to serve society most effectively.

The university should foster a plan of exchange of professorships between this institution and universities in foreign countries. I especially favor such a policy between the University of Oklahoma and similar universities in Mexico, England, France, Italy, and other European countries. This is not a novel idea. It is already in successful operation in several of our American universities. The Committee on Intellectual Co-operation under the auspices of the League of Nations and the American Student Union with headquarters in London and Paris are co-operating to bring closer affiliations between the institutions of higher learning throughout the world. The University of Oklahoma should work in close sympathy and co-operation with these agencies.

Education is under fire from many angles today. The charges include overemphasis of athletics; waste of time, money, and effort on boys and girls not interested in acquiring a college education; profitless courses of instruction; misplaced emphasis in the curricula; and numerous other indictments of more or less validity or justification. Time will not permit me to enter upon a discussion of the relative justification of these criticisms. Honesty compels us to admit that some of the criticisms are supported by undeniable facts. The acid test, of course, is the results obtained. "Education," says Arnold Bennett in a review of education in this country, "like most things except high-class cookery, must be judged by ultimate results; and though it may not be possible to pass any verdict on current educational methods, one can to a certain extent assess the values of past education by reference to the demeanor of adults who have been through it." I agree with Arnold Bennett. Education must be judged by its product. What kind of men and women are our institutions sending forth into the world? How do they differ from those who have not been exposed to this tedious process? What quality of leadership are they revealing? Do they possess community consciousness? How do they compare with other citizens in moral standards and integrity? These questions suggest some of the tests that should be applied to our educational product.

I believe there is need for a comprehensive study of educational results. Millions of dollars are now being expended for education. The public has a right to know whether they are getting value received in the form of social dividends from the enormous outlay of private and public funds. I would like to see a survey made in Oklahoma for the purpose of appraising our intellectual product.

I remind you in conclusion that the building of a great educational institution is not the task of one man. If we build a great state university in Oklahoma it will involve the united efforts of the governing board, university and state officials, faculty members, former students of the university, and the citizenship of the state. It is my sincere desire that the university shall be worthy of the confidence and the good will of our entire citizenship. I solemnly pledge my best efforts to so direct the policies of the university as to merit the moral and financial support of all those who believe in the cause of education. I shall have no divided allegiance during the time I shall serve as president of the university. My entire time and thought shall be given to the task that has been set before me.

In the administration of a complex organization like that of a great state university, I cannot hope to secure universal approval of all the things I shall do. I realize that I shall make mistakes and sometimes I shall not be able to see every problem in all its relations. But in the administration of the affairs of the university I hope to have the courage to do right, the will to be just, and the Christian virtue of being kindly, sympathetic, and open-minded. While I shall use my best efforts to increase the physical plant of this university, I am in strict accord with the fine sentiment of Van Dyke when he raised the question as to what constitutes a school and answered it as follows:

"Not ancient halls and ivy-mantled towers,
Not spacious pleasure courts,

And lofty temples of athletic fame,
　　Not fashion, nor renown
Of wealthy patronage and rich estate;
　　No, none of these can crown
A school with light and make it truly great.
　　But masters, strong and wise,
Who teach because they love the teacher's task,
　　And find their richest prize
In eyes that open and in minds that ask;
　　And boys, with heart aglow
To try their youthful vigour on their work,
　　Eager to learn and grow,
And quick to hate a coward or a shirk:
　　These constitute a school,—
A vital forge of weapons keen and bright,
　　Where living sword and tool
Are tempered for true toil or noble fight."

With this ideal of a real institution before me, I enter officially upon my solemn duties today, pledging you once for all my best efforts in behalf of the University of Oklahoma for such time as it may be my privilege to serve it.

THE STUDENT'S *ATTITUDE TOWARD* HIS *EDUCATIONAL TASK*[1]

CHAPTER TWO

I AM reminded today of God's command and promise to Abraham, recorded in the twelfth chapter and first three verses of Genesis: *Now the Lord had said unto Abraham, get thee out of the country and from thy kindred and from thy father's house, unto a land that I will show thee. And I will make of thee a great nation; and I will bless thee, and make thy name great, and thou shalt be a blessing.*

The command that came to Abraham comes to each of us sometime in life in one way or another. The time comes when we must depart from the community of our nativity. We must bid farewell to our kindred. We must leave our father's house, to go, where? "Unto a land that I will show thee." This is the experience of the youth who leaves home for the first time to enter college. He leaves a familiar environment to enter a community very unlike the one he has known. The habits of a lifetime must be changed. New friendships are to be formed, and new obligations and responsibilities are to be assumed.

A university community differs in many respects from that of the normal urban or rural community. The quiet routine of family life is to be changed for the residential

1. Convocational address delivered at the opening of the thirty-fourth academic year on September 23, 1925.

hall and the boarding house. Student activities of many kinds are to take the place of the usual pursuits in the home community. This implies that important choices are to be made and new habits are to be formed. The wisdom with which the student makes this adjustment is often a determining factor in his future success.

College life has its prosaic as well as its poetic aspects. Some hardships must be endured; some anxieties must be experienced. It goes without saying that all those who are listening to my words today will not be willing to make the sacrifices, to endure the hardships, and to meet the exacting tests of academic life. But the promises of God to Abraham are still offered to those who "endure hardness as a good soldier." The rewards of intellectual achievement are great. A name worthy of respect is assured to those who overcome the difficulties and who solve the problems incident to college life. A large opportunity for usefulness is guaranteed to all who are willing to pay the price for intellectual accomplishment.

I never stand before a great student body at the beginning of an academic year like this but what I think of all that your presence implies. In each of you is centered the hopes, the prayers, and the aspirations of parents, relatives, and friends. Your teachers back home have their eyes on you. They are expecting you to fulfill the promises of leadership and aptitude for intellectual accomplishment revealed on the playground, or in the classroom and the laboratory of your high school.

What a responsibility is this! How much of happiness or unhappiness will result from your attitude toward your work and opportunities? Will you fulfill the aspirations of your parents and justify the faith of your friends? Will you reveal the qualities of perseverance, moral courage, and devotion to duty required by exacting standards of college life? These are questions each of you must answer, and much will depend upon your decisions.

College life provides unusual opportunities for happiness. There will come to each of you the peculiar privilege of daily enjoyment of those kinds of satisfactions that cannot be secured in any other environment. The memories of the joys and pleasures that are experienced in college are those that give life its deepest satisfaction in after years. It is your high privilege, therefore, to crowd into the daily experiences of college life as much of pleasure and happiness as time will permit.

But I remind you that college life is also full of tragedies —tragedies resulting from moral battles lost, opportunities that have been passed by, and profitless expenditure of time and effort. It is well, therefore, for you to remember that you are not living for today, but for tomorrow and for the years that are ahead. Fortunate indeed is the college student who has foresight—foresight that will cause him to postpone temporary pleasures of today and devote his energies to the more serious responsibilities of the hour, in order that those more permanent joys and satisfactions may be experienced in the years to come.

The institutions of human society serve the purpose of differentiating the population into classified groups. Education is essentially a selective process. This selective process is continuous from the first grade on through the high school and into the college and through the university. At every stage of advancement pupils are revealing natural aptitudes or the lack of them. Many pupils who enter the public school never finish the primary grades; great numbers of others fall by the wayside in the progress toward the end of the high-school period; a remnant meet all the requirements of high-school tests and enter college. The mortality in the freshman year of every college and university is distressingly high, and the percentage of those that survive the entire process from the elementary school through four years of college is small indeed.

But it is the high purpose of our educational system to sift out the human product of society. Our schools and colleges are designed to test out the natural aptitudes of our young people and give direction to human effort. While the process presents its stern and unsympathetic aspects, nevertheless our educational forces have no greater duty than to make the educational process selective.

Your presence here today indicates that you have survived the intellectual and moral tests of primary and secondary schools. Many of you have given promise of mental ability to complete college, university, and professional courses by having met the academic requirements of one, two, three, or more years of college work. You are, therefore, selected lives—selected for special intellectual attainment by virtue of the mental capacities which you have revealed.

The basis of selection in this university is physical competency, intellectual aptitude, moral integrity, and spiritual efficiency. The authorities of this university, supported by its several faculties, are undertaking to apply all of these tests to every student who seeks the stamp of the institution's approval. It would make all of us happy if each of you might meet fully and satisfactorily all of the tests required in this selective process.

For all of you who give reasonable promise of fulfilling all of the requirements of university life, I wish to bid you Godspeed in the task before you. As the scholarly group in American life is relatively small, you are entitled to hearty congratulations if you can rightfully claim membership in it, for leadership in state, community enterprise, and the church is largely in the hands of the members of this group.

But your selection does not mean that you are better than

others or that you are not of the same flesh and blood as the great mass of humanity. All that is implied by mental capacities to assume intellectual and moral leadership is that larger opportunities will be open to you and corresponding responsibilities will be your lot by virtue of good inheritance and educational privileges.

I am jealous for the good name of the college-bred man. His moral and intellectual qualities should stand out. The college man should be a gentleman in the broadest and best sense of the word. He should be known for his respect for law, his observance of social proprieties, and his fineness of feeling. If our colleges and universities are unable to develop habits of self-control, inculcate into the individual the spirit of respect and reverence, and impart a sincere desire to follow the paths of righteousness, they are not fulfilling their mission to society.

I am jealous for the good name of every young woman who enrolls in our colleges and universities. Four years of college training should impart to each of them culture and refinement. The college-bred woman should possess womanliness with all that this word implies. If our colleges and universities cannot impart to the college woman the spirit of gentleness, refinement, and high ideals, they have failed to function helpfully and constructively.

I wish that the college-bred man and the college-bred woman might be recognized when they are seen on the street or appear in society. I wish that their qualities were so outstanding that they would be recognized everywhere. William James had some such thought as this in mind when he stated that "the best claim that a college education can possibly make on your respect, the best thing it can aspire to accomplish for you is this; that it shall help you to know a good man when you see him."

The presence here of this great student body raises some

[24]

questions that each one of you should answer very definitely for yourself. What is your purpose in coming to the university? What do you expect to do while you are here? Are you willing to pay the price in time and effort in order to acquire an education? Have you definitely decided to conform to the reasonable requirements of college regulations? These are questions that demand an answer by you. Upon a wise answer will depend your happiness here, as well as the general direction of your life purposes in the years that are to come.

The answers to these questions were reasonably simple in past years. Formerly there was no reason to enter college except for the purpose of acquiring knowledge, intellectual power, or skill in some chosen field of effort. But the mere presence of a student in college today does not always imply that the essential aim is that of acquiring a college education. There is no denying the fact that the motive of many students for entering college is a complex one. The increasing complexities of college life account for this fact. The interests of college students have greatly multiplied in recent years. The social life in college and university has become increasingly attractive. Athletics now has a great appeal to many students. Student organizations offer opportunities for preferment and leadership. It is not unnatural that many students should be attracted to college because of these unusual and recent opportunities for self-expression that were unknown in the college life of a generation ago.

But we must not forget that the essential and primary purpose of entering college or university is to acquire an academic, technical, or professional education. Our colleges and universities have been established for this essential purpose. State-supported institutions like the University of Oklahoma have been established by the taxpayers for this single purpose. The taxpayers are unwilling to provide funds for the maintenance of educational institutions merely to provide an opportunity for a social career for our young people, or to provide a place for leisure to those who want to avoid work under their parents' direction at home.

Students must never get into the habit of taking the educational facilities that the taxpayers have provided for them as a matter of course. You must not assume that the facilities provided here are merely for your enjoyment. Educational opportunity in this university is not free; it is costing the taxpayers of this state a considerable sum of money. The fact that your parents are not required to pay the cost of your education here does not indicate that it is free. For that reason no student can afford to utilize the time of professors and occupy space in classrooms and laboratories if it is not his serious purpose to make the most of the opportunities that the people of this state have provided here.

John Tyndall, in an address to the students of University College, London, delivered about thirty years ago, declared that "the object of education is, or ought to be, to provide wise exercise for the student's capacity, wise direction for his tendencies, and through this exercise and this direction to furnish his mind with such knowledge as may contribute to the usefulness, the beauty, and the nobleness of life."

Charles A. Dana once said in an address to the students of Union College that there were three things essential to education: "First, that one shall see what he looks at, in all its qualities, distinctions, perspectives, and relations, and be able to think about it intelligently. Second, that he shall be able to communicate his vision and his thoughts about it with accuracy, force, and grace. Third, that he shall know how to find out what he needs to know, being able to locate and depend exclusively upon the reliable sources of information."

John Palmer Gavit, in his recent book entitled *College*, which is the finest survey of college problems that has appeared in many years, says: "The education needed in the days before us is an education calculated to fit men to live together, to work together and to understand themselves and each other and their diverse individual, mutual, and common problems as they arise in the intricate, incessant interplay of life; to understand and utilize, too, the environment in which that life must be lived . . . . . Before anything worth while is written something must be done, something must be lived! . . . . The aim of education all along the line, and unceasing from the cradle to the grave, will be to train Thinkers who Do; Doers who Think. The two kinds of activity cannot be separated without disaster. The Thinker who knows nothing of Doing is no guide for anyone; the Doer who has not learned to Think is no safer. The fact is that only through Doing can one learn rightly to Think. Through definite activities, useful in their own right and evidently respectable because they are useful, as well as through the written records of doing and thinking in the past, and talking and listening to talk, and reflection upon these, the student of any age gains that cultivation of all of himself which develops the intelligence which is nothing more or less than all of himself."

The confusion of motives for going to college is brilliantly described by Dr. Alexander Meiklejohn in his inaugural address as president of Amherst, in 1922: "The college is a good place for making friends; it gives excellent experience in getting on with men; it has exceptional advantages as an athletic club; it is a relatively safe place for a boy when he first leaves home; on the whole it may improve a student's manners; it gives acquaintance with lofty ideals of character, preaches the doctrine of social service, exalts the virtues and duties of citizenship. All these conceptions seem to the teacher to hide or to obscure the fact that college is fundamentally a place of the mind, a time for thinking, an opportunity of knowing."

Dr. Meiklejohn in this quotation clearly differentiates between the primary and secondary motives that should characterize the student in college today. This distinguished educator is essentially correct in emphasizing the fact that "the college is fundamentally a place of the mind, a time for thinking, an opportunity for knowing." The more clearly you conceive of these objectives as the essential purposes for being here, the more completely will you be able to justify the sacrifices that have been made by the citizenship of this state in providing for the educational facilities that exist on this campus.

It is well for you to recall today that after all is said a great student body like this is a cross section of the youth of the state. I am sure there are enrolled in this institution at this hour students that are typical of every element of the population of Oklahoma. There are those of earnest purpose and fixed convictions; there are some who are indifferent to moral obligations and unaware of what these privileges imply.

"No one in close touch with American education," said President Lowell on one occasion, "has failed to notice the lack among the mass of undergraduates of keen interest in their studies and the small regard for scholarly attainment." This is true because students are coming up to our colleges and universities in enormous numbers, and it is probably more than we have a right to expect that all of them would come with a passion for seeking truth and the moral purpose to meet the exacting requirements of college life.

It is not surprising, therefore, that in every student body we find the loafer, the cribber, the habitual borrower, the social dandy, the chronic kicker, and the intellectual parasite. I do not believe that the aggregate number of these is more than a negligible element in any student population. But probably there is no college or university community in the country that does not have representatives of each. I certainly hope the number of undesirables that may come under one or the other of these classifications may prove to be negligible in the student body of this university.

We are today entering upon the thirty-fourth academic year of the University of Oklahoma. The enrolment in the university through the years has grown from a relatively small student body to a comparatively large student enrolment. The university is recognized as one of the important educational institutions of the country.

But you are reminded that physical equipment and financial resources will not alone make a really great university. Greatness is reflected in the quality of the scholarship, ideals, and consecration of the men and women who administer the affairs of the university and who fill the chairs in the several colleges and professional schools of the institution. *No university can be great unless the student body can be brought to appreciate the opportunities and caused to make the best possible use of the facilities provided for them.* If I am correct in these assertions, the greatness of this university is essentially in our hands. It is your responsibility and mine to give this university its place of commanding influence among the institutions of higher education in the United States.

Ralph Waldo Emerson, in his Phi Beta Kappa address at Cambridge, in 1837, declared that "the day is always his who works in it with serenity and great aims." In another connection in the same address he said, "give me insight into today, and you may have all the antique and future worlds." These promises may find fulfillment in the life of each of you if you keep your eyes on the stars and follow in the pathway of truth. To those of you who question your strength, who fear the steep ascent to the mountain top of your ambitions, I invite you to listen to the prophetic words of one of America's most popular poets:

"Trust in thine own untried capacity
　As thou wouldst trust in God himself.
　　　Thy soul
　Is but an emanation from the whole.

"Thou does not dream what forces lie in thee,
　Vast and unfathomed as the grandest sea.
　Thy silent mind o'er diamond caves may roll;
　Go seek them, but let pilot Will control
　Those passions which thy favoring winds can be.

"No man shall place a limit to thy strength;
　Such triumphs as no mortal ever gained
　May yet be thine if thou wilt but believe
　In thy Creator and thyself. At length,
　Some feet will tread all heights now unattained—
　Why not thine own? Press on; achieve! achieve!"

On behalf of the several faculties of the university, I wish for each of you the largest measure of success and happiness during this year. To the freshmen entering the university for the first time, I assure you of a sympathetic environment if you have come here for the high purpose of acquiring a knowledge of essential truth. To those of you who have come to love this beautiful campus and these classic halls through past contact with the university, I wish for each of you the greatest measure of satisfaction as you enter upon the work of another year.

EDUCATION AND THE USEFUL LIFE[1]

CHAPTER THREE

ACROSS the front of Langdell Hall, one of the historic buildings devoted to legal instruction at Harvard University, is this inscription: "Thou shall teach them ordinances and laws and shall show them the way in which they must walk and the work that they must do." This sentence is taken from Exod. 18:20. As one reads these words today they seem to reflect a trace of the Puritan spirit of an earlier period, but to my mind this verse from the Bible might appropriately be made the motto of any institution of higher learning.

The high purpose of every college or university is to impart a knowledge of the laws that govern our social relations, of the ethical principles that should guide our conduct, and to prepare each student for the work he should do in the world. This passage of Scripture is a summary of education and the useful life. I would emphasize this truth as we begin the work of a new year in this university.

It is important to keep in mind the reasons for our being here. To express the thought more precisely, it is important for us to understand the reasons for the state of Oklahoma establishing this institution. It is well for all of us to recall that the taxpayers support this institution on the theory that those who accept the advantages offered here expect

1. Convocational address delivered at the opening of the thirty-fifth academic year on September 22, 1926.

[31]

to make the most of these facilities and return to the state in future years both interest and principal in terms of productive achievements. Students must not get the notion that this institution and these facilities are free. Education is expensive, and the more advanced the instruction the greater the cost. In reality you are being awarded today a scholarship that is valued at $300.00—for that is approximately the per capita cost of instruction—on the theory that those who accept the benefits provided will utilize these facilities of instruction in the most profitable way. For any student to accept the educational advantages here without assuming the obligations to prove worthy of the confidence imposed by the citizenship of the state would be nothing short of dishonest.

The serious task before the faculties of the university is to make intelligent and reflective men and women out of all those who have enrolled. I am fully aware that many students enter college with rather vague notions as to what it is all about. It goes without saying that in this day and time not all students enrol in college for the essential purpose of acquiring an education. It is probably more accurate to say that the motive that prompts most students to enter upon a college career is a complex one. Social advantages, fraternal opportunities, athletics, and the acquisition of knowledge, all enter into consideration. It becomes, therefore, the difficult task of those who administer or instruct to develop discrimination on the part of the student in the use of his time.

It is regrettable that so many students come up to college with so little real intellectual interest. Some come with a real distaste for scholarship. This is largely due to the student's misconception of scholarship. He often identifies a scholar with scholastic affectation, and learning is supposed to be synonymous with pedantry. It is not surprising, therefore, that young people enter college with distorted notions and misplaced interest when such widely read authors as H. G. Wells proclaim to the world that our educational institutions are "baseball and football universities, where every sort of intellectual activity is subordinated to a main business of attracting, boarding and amusing our adolescence."

The pursuit of knowledge is the most natural activity of man. Boswell reports Dr. Johnson as saying: "A desire of knowledge is the natural feeling of mankind; and every human being, whose mind is not debased, will be willing to give all that he has, to get knowledge." William Ellery Channing, in an eloquent address on the scientific and intellectual tendencies of the first half of the nineteenth century, declared that "every mind was made for growth, for knowledge; and its nature is sinned against, when it is doomed to ignorance." Although more than half a century in time and three thousand miles of ocean waste separate the authors of these statements, both the learned Dr. Johnson and the eloquent Channing express the same doctrine of man's eternal hunger for knowledge.

The relation of knowledge to man's happiness is nowhere so forcibly expressed as in these familiar words recorded in Proverbs:

"Happy is the man that findeth wisdom, and the man that getteth understanding.
For the merchandise of it is better than the merchandise of silver, and the gain thereof than fine gold.
She is more precious than rubies; and all things thou canst desire are not to be compared unto her.
Wisdom is the principal thing; therefore, get wisdom; and with all thy getting get understanding."

I am wondering if all this sounds trite. Does it appear

[33]

merely to be the rattling of the dry bones of a dead philosophy? I hope not, for this is not an overstatement of the relation of knowledge to happiness. Neither is it an extravagant appraisal of the relative value of wisdom. This doctrine is basic to the task before us. I presume that many of you have come to the university with high hopes of your social opportunities. I hope that you have come also with equal anticipations of the intellectual advantages that are available to you. Be that as it may, let me emphatically declare to you that to impart knowledge that may ripen into wisdom and to get understanding that may contribute to rational living are the essential and predominating purposes of all effort here.

My hope for this university is that it may be known as a place where students work hard. Above all else, I hope it may merit this reputation. There is a widespread opinion that many students enter college to avoid hard work. There are still some parents who think that the object of acquiring a college education is to enable their children to avoid labor. There is no greater reflection upon the good name of any educational institution than that it is a place where laziness is tolerated and where students get the impression that the object of education is to relieve them from work. I agree heartily with Bertrand Russell when he says in his recent book, *Education and the Good Life*, that "no one should be admitted to college unless he satisfies the test of ability, and no one should be allowed to remain unless he satisfies the authorities that he is using his time to advantage. The idea of the university as a place of leisure where rich young men loaf for three or four years is dying, but, like Charles II, it is an unconscionable time about it." I accept this doctrine and we shall try to subscribe to it in this university.

Some years ago Dr. Richard C. Cabot, a professor in the

Harvard Medical School, wrote a rather remarkable book which he called *What Men Live By*. He concluded that work, play, love and worship are essential to life's satisfactions. "Personality, decency," says Cabot, "and all that is human in us grows up through selection. By the choice of work, of play, of companions, of words, people are made what they are." This is a profound truth. It applies with great force to students. College life offers a wide range of choices in the development of personality. The tragedy of it all is that so many college students make such poor choices. The larger freedom incident to college life gives an opportunity to choose between effective work on the one hand or debasing idleness on the other; of wholesome plays or sinful diversions; of stimulating friendships or association with the depraved and irresponsible; of the choice of language expressive of the noblest thoughts of the best minds or the use of the jargon of the wharf rat or the profanity of the groom.

The place of work in the life of college students needs emphasis. Let us have no misunderstanding about the nature of the learning process. There is no easy road to high intellectual attainment or to the best preparation for life's duties and responsibilities. Our colleges and universities must not inculcate a false philosophy of life by making the daily task of the student too easy. My sincere desire for this university is that it may be known as a place where students are expected to meet exacting standards of preparation for the subjects they are pursuing. If any of you have come to this university with any false idea about the relative importance of work and recreation, my hope is that for your good it may be speedily dispelled by those who direct your intellectual endeavors.

What, after all, is the real purpose of our colleges and universities? Answers to this question have been attempted many times. But the question persists and, in recent times, it is being repeated more often and with greater emphasis. Robert Herrick, the popular American author, is one of the latest to raise this question and to attempt an answer in his novel entitled *Chimes*. Is it "to attract students," says he, "by athletics and fraternity houses, who hope to mount from one social stratum to a little higher one, thanks to these college associations? Or is it for those who desire to follow the long, hard road of science and scholarship to keep alight the sacred fires of learning?" One would judge that "Eureka University," the fictitious title given by Herrick to the institution that he describes, does not come under the latter classification; but Herrick makes a contribution to the educational thought of the times in the following words taken from his book:

"Yet scholarship to be enduring must be creative, must be based on all human faculties, emotional as well as mental . . . . . Learning to become productive must have within it the vital star, compact of perception and imagination: must be creative." While there is in this generalization a slight confusion of psychological terms, at the same time there is the essential idea of the function of a true university.

For some reason our institutions with rare exceptions have not contributed largely to the enduring type of scholarship. It is difficult to decide whether this is due to standards of instruction, organization of curricula or to the preparation and viewpoint of the student. In such books as the *Plastic Age* and *Gray Towers* we have a biased and abnormal view of college life. The fact is that college students are probably neither better nor worse morally than those of a generation ago. They are certainly coming up to college with better preparation for their work but their habits have changed, their outlook upon life is different and it seems that our institutions have not quite made the necessary readjustments in organization to meet this changing situation. We all are inclined to agree with the anonymous author of *Gray Towers* that "college training ought to develop correct mental habits, make for standards and a sense of values. If all university trained people had the foundation of the large, important facts in the different branches of knowledge, think how much richer social contacts would be." Every word of this is true, and I take it for granted that every college or university worthy of the name is earnestly striving to that end.

Intellectuals continue to blast at the foundations of the temple of learning. It has become a popular sport and pastime, more fascinating for the intellectual American than golf and for the Englishman than cricket. Mr. Wells, who is always interesting, often plausible, but rarely convincing, contends in an article in the September (1926) *Cosmopolitan* that the four years at college are wasted and prophesies that the time will come when Oxford, Cambridge, Yale and Harvard will stand empty and clean for the sightseeing tourist. Mr. Wells is careful not to indicate very definitely when this catastrophe will come upon the world. I believe the late Charles W. Eliot is a better authority on the work and the future of our educational institutions than H. G. Wells. In his book *A Late Harvest*, which contains miscellaneous papers written by this distinguished American between eighty and ninety, he says: "Now, it has happened to me to witness and take active part in the development of American education from 1854 to the present day; and the strongest conviction I have derived from this long survey is that the improvement of American education, from top to bottom; from the kindergarten through the professional school, during these sixty-seven years is in high degree encouraging and hopeful."

When Wells turns from speculation to reason he gets on safer ground. In another connection in the article to which

I refer, he says: "There are millions of people, half educated and uneducated, vividly aware that they are ill informed and uneducated, passionately eager to learn and to acquire a sense of purpose and validity." In another connection he says: "Much absolute rubbish is fed to this great hunger, and still more adulterated food. This appetite, which should grow with what it feeds upon, is thwarted and perverted."

This is true but it is not new. Two explanations of the failure of our institutions to educate thoroughly those who seek educational advantages are offered. A noted French educator, who was recently an exchange professor at Yale, suggests that the ineffectiveness of education is due to the fact that our students are being trained *to learn rather than to think*. Herrick in *Chimes*, to which I have previously referred, traces it to the system of courses and credits. "Courses vary widely," says he, "in their educational content, as the minds of the instructors who give them, their standard of accomplishment, and the care with which they impose their standards—and yet all count the same in the educational banking house." You who have read Olive Deane Hormel's *Co-Ed* will recall that this thought runs entirely through her book. I am frank to say that I believe the time has come when our present system of courses and credits must be modified. The great diversity in content of courses and standards of instruction make this inevitable. There is too much talk among college students of "snap" or "crip" courses. If there is any justification whatever for the charge made by one of the authors whom I have quoted that in many institutions fraternities keep lists of courses for the information of their pledges that are regarded as easy to pass, there is need for a thorough evaluation of all courses that students are permitted to elect. There is even a greater need for administrative authorities to work out some better plan of relative credits based upon content and standards of instruction.

The highest usefulness in life for the individual is threatened today by an unbalanced attitude toward academic and technical instruction. There has been a tendency in recent years to interpret vocational education in too narrow terms. The process of delimiting the scope of knowledge should come slowly. Concentration within a narrow field of interest should be built gradually upon a broad foundation of general knowledge. "Professional training," says Professor Whitehead in his great book on *Science and the Modern World*, "can only touch one side of education. Its center of gravity lies in the intellect, and its chief tool is the printed book. The center of gravity of the other side of training should lie in intuition without an analytical divorce from the total environment." This is a wise generalization. Life's greatest usefulness is only promised to those who best balance in their educational training the knowledge of the theoretical and the practical.

But I confess that it is much easier to state this principle than to apply it. *Education has become a rather irrational pursuit of an imaginary intellectual goal through a morass of bewildering facts.* Science is daily extending the boundaries of truth. Differentiation of subject matter is going on endlessly. No mind can comprehend it all. What are our educational institutions doing about it? Aristotle, Comte and Spencer, each, attempted a synthesis of all knowledge but that will not be undertaken again. The scope of knowledge is too great today and its elements are too diverse.

But a perspective of knowledge seems to point one way out of the difficulty. The relative importance of the facts of science and the appraisal of their practical consequences are within the range of human accomplishment. It is basic to adequate instruction. No instructor has done his task well who does not guide his students on the pathway of learning by the great signposts of truth.

Herbert Spencer raised the question as to what knowledge is of most worth and attempted to answer it. Spencer's answer might not be adequate today but everyone who undertakes to direct the intellectual progress of students should keep this question constantly in mind and undertake to answer it in the light of the background of the subject matter of instruction.

When we turn from the processes of learning to the students' mental reaction to the larger interests of college life, we are confronted today with a new problem; namely, that of divided loyalties. We talk much these days about college spirit and college loyalty. A simple analysis of student attitudes reveals the fact that loyalty is not a unified product. Students are tempted to divide their loyalty between their particular school; their fraternity or sorority, if they are affiliated with a Greek-letter organization of this kind; and various other types of organizations that compose the complex life of the present day college or university student.

Two or three questions naturally arise when we think of the allegiance of college students. What is the psychological effect of divided loyalties? Are these loyalties accumulative, paradoxical or antagonistic? Are loyalties to social organizations or particular schools nullifying the larger loyalty to the institutions that foster these minor activities? These are questions that need to be answered. Their importance becomes more significant with the increase in the complexities of university life. There should be no conflict of loyalty between the larger interest of the university and those of the organizations that are subsidiary to it. Social groups within the larger circle of university life should be so co-ordinated that the loyalty fostered by one would never be dissociated from the larger loyalty of the other. It would

[40]

certainly result disastrously if the time should ever come when the divided loyalties of college students should have the effect of destroying the more important loyalty to the university.

This is not merely an academic question. It is a question that must be answered in the future. Just as our loyalty to our town and our state should not cause us to be less loyal to our country, neither should our loyalty to our fraternity or other social group make us less loyal to the university that gives existence to these minor social groups.

This reminds me to raise the question of what students mean by college spirit. We talk much these days about this rather indefinite influence in college life and I wonder sometimes if we have a clear understanding as to what this thing we call college spirit really is. I observe occasionally that some students who yell the loudest at "pep" meetings are not the most sensitive to student honor. It sometimes happens that after great student rallies or great athletic victories some students go out and conduct themselves in a manner that brings reproach upon the good name of the institution whose athletic victories have brought joy to their hearts. Of course, these are exceptional cases; but I am compelled to believe that students of this type have a perverted notion of college spirit.

To my mind college spirit is an expression of loyalty. We rejoice over athletic victories not because an opposing team has gone down in defeat, but rather because our team has reflected the loftiest qualities of perseverance, team work, and fair play that are inculcated in the life of the institution. We manifest college spirit when our debating teams win over competitors, when some student or group of students reveal unusual talents in this field or that, or when a student group takes a strong and courageous moral stand against wrongdoing.

Student loyalty is reflected in the observance of social

proprieties. The normal relations that people bear to each other today is the result of ages of conflict and suffering. The method of trial and error has been repeatedly applied until the best form of human conduct has been evolved. As a result of all these experiences we have learned certain things that we should do and that should not be done. We know that when we violate what we call moral principles sooner or later embarrassment, grief or suffering must result.

Students, therefore, should observe these social proprieties; boys and girls should observe them in their relations to each other. The student who ridicules or ignores the well-established social traditions reveals mental and moral deficiencies. A university community is no place for a young man or young woman of this type.

It was John Ruskin who said that "the entire object of true education is to make people not merely do the right thing, but enjoy right things." The University of Oklahoma is committed to this academic dualism. May you be willing to give all that you have of time and effort to this task. I admonish you

> "If you have hard work to do,
>   Do it now.
> Today the skies are clear and blue,
> Tomorrow clouds may come in view,
> Yesterday is not for you;
>   Do it now."

My plea in closing is not to procrastinate. This is the besetting sin of most students. Do the things that need to be done and do them now is my earnest admonition. Keep the ideal of a useful life before you as you perform your daily tasks here. I commend to you finally the philosophy of Robert Whitaker:

"Live for something, have a purpose
        And that purpose keep in view;
Drifting like a helmless vessel,
Thou canst ne'er to life be true.
Half the wrecks that strew life's ocean,
        If some star had been their guide,
Might have now been riding safely,
        But they drifted with the tide.

"Live for something—God and angels
        Are thy watchers in the strife,
And above the smoke and conflict
        Gleams the victor's crown of life.
Live for something; God has given
        Freely of His stores divine;
Richest gifts of earth and heaven,
        If thou willest, may be thine."

THE COMRADESHIP OF LEARNING[1]

CHAPTER FOUR

I NEVER stand before a great college group like this at the beginning of a new year without thinking of the great number of people whose interests are centered here. This is a great student group—the largest that ever assembled on this campus at a formal opening of the academic year. Within the reach of my voice are hundreds of students from Oklahoma. I presume every county and almost every city, town and village is represented by one or more students. There are students here from many states and a few from foreign countries. Every one of you is the representative of a family group who are sacrificing much that you might share the opportunities provided by the university. In you are centered the hopes and prayers of your loved ones at home. You represent, also, a high school where you prepared for college. Your teachers are vitally concerned about your fulfilling the promise of making good in your academic work. The university, therefore, becomes today a center of influence that far transcends the boundaries of our campus. As we assemble for a new year's work we must never forget that the invisible ties of love and friendship reach to every section of Oklahoma, to many states and even across the seas.

Since the opening convocation one year ago approximately 6,400 students have enrolled and pursued courses in

1. Convocational address delivered at the opening of the thirty-sixth academic year on September 21, 1927.

[44]

this university during the regular and summer terms. Seven hundred and seventy-one students have completed their work for some degree during the same period. These young men and young women have gone out from the university to take their places in the business and professional life of the state and nation. We are missing familiar faces this morning—men and women who took an active part in the various activities of college life during recent years. This means, of course, that the beginning of every academic year differs from all preceding years. Familiar faces and names fade out of the picture; new faces and new names appear. New leadership emerges as leaders of other days go elsewhere. The responsibility that rests upon you who are entering the university for the first time or who are returning to resume your studies is to see that there is someone to assume the responsibilities that have been laid down by those who have gone on before you.

The great commonwealth of Oklahoma has expressed its faith in your earnestness of purpose and potential qualities of mind and heart by providing these buildings and making available these scholarly men and women for your instruction without cost to you. You are to be congratulated on opportunities that are before you. Many of you are permitted to enjoy these advantages as a result of the sacrifices of your parents. As I welcome you to the university, I earnestly admonish you at the same time to make the best use of your college days, justify the faith that your parents have manifested in you, and prove that you are worthy of the benefactions of the collective citizenship of this state.

I realize that there is a wide range of difference in intellectual outlook and moral purpose in every student group of this kind. You are fortunate if you have entered college with an abiding intellectual interest and a definite purpose. I hope many of you have already acquired a love of learning, but I fear that many of you are here with uncertain purposes and without much comprehension of what is involved in acquiring a college education. No doubt some of you have come not for the primary purpose of acquiring an education. If you belong to this group, I admonish you at once to begin the important task of finding out what are the essential things and what are the nonessentials in college life.

The first task of every student who really seeks a college education is to develop an interest in things intellectual. The abiding satisfactions of intellectual pursuits are dependent upon one's ability to enjoy the conquests of learning. I pity the student who comes to college with the thought that classroom lectures, laboratory exercises and assigned readings in the library are things to be endured between weekend parties and social diversions. There is a place in college life for social activities of many kinds, but they are incidental and secondary to the high purpose of intellectual pursuits.

But something more than intellectual interest is required for a successful college career. Intellectual interest must be strongly supported by a high moral purpose. Everett Dean Martin says in his book on *The Meaning of a Liberal Education* that "education has one thing in common with religion. One must come to it with clean hands and a pure heart or one can never know the secret power in it." I subscribe to this doctrine. The rewards of intellectual accomplishment are held out only to those who possess the qualities of perseverance, high aspiration, intellectual honesty, love of truth and humility of spirit.

The gateway of intellectual opportunity is closed to those deficient in moral qualities. Character and culture are not synonymous terms but the possession of one implies the appropriation of the other. I am not contending that the morally deficient cannot acquire facts, but encyclopedic

[46]

knowledge is not learning. Learning implies the assimilation of facts and the appropriation and utilization of the best heritage of the past.

My thorough belief in this doctrine causes me to hope that no one will enter into this comradeship of learning who does not possess the basic quality of integrity. That no one may misunderstand my meaning, I will attempt to express my thought in specific terms. It is expected that every prospective student who enrols in this university will obey the laws of his country; respect the rights of his fellow students; live a clean, moral life; make reasonable preparation for his daily work; and avoid sham and pretense in his relations with others. This university has nothing to offer those who are not willing to subscribe to this moral code.

It is important that you get a proper perspective of college life at the beginning. If you succeed here, you must distinguish between the essential and the nonessential. There will be many claims upon your time. These demands range all the way from the most important academic requirements to the most frivolous social engagements. If you are to succeed in college, you must provide adequate time for the essential things and frankly assign to social diversion a secondary place.

Much unhappiness results from students laying too much emphasis on unimportant things. They are inclined to give too much value to the irrelevant and nonessentials in college life. I am convinced that many students appraise membership in social organizations in college too highly. This tendency has resulted in the overorganization of student activities. I am convinced that we have too many student organizations. I do not doubt that a thorough survey would show that there is much overlapping of function and needless absorption of student time in organizations that could reasonably be dispensed with in college life. I believe that this problem merits the most careful scrutiny on the part of college and university officials.

I believe, frankly, that many students overemphasize the importance of membership in a fraternity or a sorority. This was quite in evidence during the days of "rushing" last week in this university. Many students were greatly disappointed because they did not get a bid to membership in some sorority or fraternity. Some took this matter so seriously as to consider leaving school. To my mind this is an indication that many students place too much importance on acquiring membership in a Greek-letter organization.

This reminds me that there is need for radical reform in the rushing rules in the university. There is something radically wrong about a system that encourages five times as many students to accept the courtesies incident to rush week as can possibly be extended invitations to join a Greek-letter organization. I hope before another year a more rational system can be worked out. I pledge to our fraternities and sororities the hearty co-operation of university authorities in the solution of this problem.

Many students are entering our colleges and universities today who have not acquired habits of work. In fact, it is believed by many people that great numbers of students enrol in college to avoid honest work in some useful vocation. There is no denying the fact that every college has its loafing contingent.

It is the duty of our educational institutions to inculcate right habits on the part of the students. The time has not come, and probably will never come, when civilization can be sustained without work. Certainly no student can acquire a real education without hard and sustained work. There is no eight-hour day for those who seek real intellectual accomplishment. To hold out hopes of a diploma and a degree to any student for four years of indifferent pursuit of knowledge is sinful. No one should be ignorant of the heights to climb and the difficulty of the journey that leads to the mountain peak of knowledge.

I want the University of Oklahoma to bear the reputation, and to merit it, of being a place where honest work is required and where no rewards are bestowed except for meritorious accomplishment.

This reminds me to say that education has developed some false connotations in recent years. We have come to use the term "education" very loosely. "Almost any method of salesmanship," says a scholarly writer, "or trick of influencing people for any ends whatever is now 'education.' Everyone educates the public. It is marvelous how large a portion of the population of these states is qualified to instruct. Education has become the game men perpetually work to convert their neighbors. It is the cure for every social ill. How shall we put an end to the crime wave, abolish war, how to prevent social revolution—or bring revolution about—how induce unwilling people to accept cheerfully the coercion of national prohibition or give lip service to some one's favorite brand of patriotism? The answer is in all cases—education. If you are engaged in increasing the sale of a certain soap, in putting everyone on guard against the social disability of which one's best friend will not tell him, if you can frighten a multitude with the danger of pyorrhea and thus increase your profit in tooth paste—all this is now called education." Probably this loose use of the word results from the passion of our people for education. However, the time has come when we should restrict the use of the word to its rightful place.

Samuel McChord Crothers, the genial philosopher and author, says: "In the exuberant hospitality of America, if a person wants anything he has only to ask for it. Whether he gets it, is another matter; he will at least get something with

the same name." This is equally true of educational subjects as of apothecary remedies. If a student wants anything
when he comes to college, all he has to do is to ask for it.
He may not get what he asks for, but he will get a course
by the same name. He may think he is getting a course
with real content, conducted by a competent teacher who
inspires and guides the student through the intricacies and
difficulties of the subject; but instead he may get a "crip
course" with no objective, ill-defined subject matter, and
taught by a teacher devoid of the spirit of scholarship. But
in either alternative, we call it education. It is not surprising,
under the circumstances, that the marketing of the new
brand of tooth paste and a laboratory course in genetics or
a seminar in history should be called education.

I do not think the time will ever come when all courses
offered in our colleges and universities will be exactly equal
in content or standards of instruction. I do believe that an
honest effort should be made not only to evaluate the
courses on the basis of content and number of hours of classroom work required, but also to take into consideration the
quality of instruction in determining the relative amount of
credit to be given. There is much truth in the statement of
Everett Dean Martin, whom I have previously quoted,
when he says that "while much of the demand for education
is genuine and spontaneous, much of it is spurious, irrelevant, inconsequential. The increased attendance at school
or university does not necessarily mean that more education
is going on. It is frequently said that our colleges are crowded
with inferior students. Athletics, fraternities and the automobile tend to displace science and the classics. American
youth has acquired its ideal of college life from the motion
pictures."

There is no question that the sources of knowledge are
more varied today than ever before. The motion picture is

only one of these numerous agencies that supply the sources of knowledge, but as these sources multiply the accuracy of the knowledge correspondingly decreases. We certainly know more things today than we ever knew before; but, unfortunately, we know too many things that are not so. An American writer facetiously describes a school that he found in an unfrequented section of London, over the door of which appeared these words: "The Anglo-American School of Polite Unlearning." In referring to this institution, he says we have many very good institutions of learning but there is need of a school for the "benefit of persons who are desirous, not so much of learning, as being assisted to unlearn a number of things that are not good for them."

I do not think we need independent institutions for this purpose, but it is certainly the function of every institution of higher learning to correct erroneous views and substitute truth for falsehood in the thinking of students.

It is difficult to free our minds from superstition, prejudice and provincialism. It is often necessary to unlearn many things before real knowledge can be imparted. The teacher of high purpose has no more important task than helping the student correct false impressions acquired through the years from irresponsible sources of information. But there are still a good many of what Carlyle describes in his *Sartor Resartus* as Professors of Things in General. We still laugh at Gneschen who got his geography and history mixed by declaring to his teacher that Caesar swam the Nile, yet kept his commentaries dry. But this joke grows more serious when we bring it nearer home and recall that an instructor in an American college explained to his student in answer to an inquiry that Low German had reference to those people living in the valleys, and High German was a term used to describe the Germanic people who lived in the mountain regions.

We have heard much in recent years about academic freedom. Certainly a university should foster intellectual honesty and independent thinking, but academic freedom implies an obligation to think rigidly and to announce opinions of consequence only after careful deliberation and thorough investigation. It is as much a virtue to be intolerant of loose thinking as to be tolerant of the opinions that differ from our own. Most of the prejudice against scholarship has resulted from loose thinking and immature judgments on the part of so-called scholars.

Professor John Dewey describes education as a process of freeing the mind of "bunk." This is a difficult undertaking. "Strive as we may," says one educational authority, "to eradicate it, there is always in our thinking an amount of error, of wish-fancy accepted as objective fact, of exaggeration, special pleading, self-justification."

John Galsworthy tells us somewhere of a bootmaker who inscribed over the door of his shop: *Mens conscia recti* (a mind conscious of right). That would be an appropriate motto for all of us who would guide the intellectual course of the youth of the land along sure paths of truth and virtue.

We are entering today upon what promises to be the most successful year in the history of the university. A generous people has made it possible to provide increased facilities for doing our work. A number of men and women of high scholastic attainments have joined our teaching staff for the first time. The spirit of the university probably was never better than it is today. The relations between faculty members and students are free and cordial. Under these happy circumstances, we should go forward on the conquest of learning with great enthusiasm and confidence.

Bliss Carmen has beautifully said that:

"Three things are given man to do—
To dare, to labor and to grow:
Not otherwise from earth we came,
Nor otherwise our ways we go."

In the spirit of this philosophy, let us enter upon our work. The comradeship of learning involves the spirit of courage and labor. Growth in body, mind and soul will be the rewards for your efforts. With these high purposes, let us unite our efforts in making this a year of great intellectual triumphs and fine companionship.

THE SPIRIT OF *ADVENTURE* IN

LEARNING[1]

CHAPTER FIVE

THE SPIRIT of adventure has characterized the pursuit of knowledge in all ages. The quest of knowledge is a record of courageous deeds and persistent effort. The devoted truth-seeker has ever found a thrill in his explorations of the unknown. Jason's quest of the Golden Fleece and Sir Galahad's search for the Holy Grail were inspired by the conscious limitations of knowledge. Their exploits differ only in detail from those of Galileo searching for the laws of natural phenomena, Sir William Herschel's survey of the skies in search of a new planet, Swammerdam's pursuit of the life history of insects, and Millikan's quest of cosmic rays.

The results of the adventurous spirit in science have often been of more significance than decisive battles and treaties of peace between nations. One has merely changed geographical boundaries, while the other has changed the range of human reckoning and extended the limits of knowledge. "A generation ago," says J. B. S. Haldane, "the earliest date known with any certainty was that of the first Olympic Game in 776 B. C." Historical research has recently extended our knowledge back at least to 1915 B. C.

1. Convocational address delivered at the opening of the thirty-seventh academic year on September 19, 1928.

[54]

Astronomical science has given us a new unit for stellar space. It is the parsec, a unit of eighteen billion miles. Multiples of this unit are necessary today to encompass the scope of man's knowledge of the universe. The research of the geologist, the biologist, the chemist, the physicist and the astronomer has extended the scope of the intellectual man's world to limits inconceivable even a century ago. The achievements of these intellectual explorers constitute a record characterized by high adventure, persistent effort and great courage.

It is well for us this morning, as we enter upon a year's work in pursuit of knowledge, to recall, briefly, the experiences and accomplishments of a few of the men who have changed the world's intellectual horizon by virtue of their contributions to human knowledge. It was Galileo, a young professor at the University of Pisa, who climbed the spiral staircase of the Leaning Tower one morning in 1591, and from the seventh tier of arches dropped two balls of unequal weight and demonstrated to his skeptical associates the apparently paradoxical law of falling bodies.

In the year that Galileo died Sir Isaac Newton was born. He not only explained the motions of the planets and their satellites, but his discovery of the laws of gravitation established the universe upon the principle of natural law. Albert Einstein has given new applications to Newton's laws by advancing the theory that space is curved and that all motion is relative. Can you imagine the satisfaction that has come to this great scientist to have his fellow-workers in this field verify his theory by their observations of the eclipse of some of the heavenly bodies?

Who has not been thrilled by the brilliant researches of Michael Faraday in the field of electro-magnetism, whose accomplishments have given us a new world of light and power?

The life of Louis Pasteur reads like a romance. The story

of his five years' search for a specific for rabies is a romantic chapter in the history of science. Love of knowledge and the joy of discovery caused Dr. Lazear in 1900 to permit himself to be bitten by a mosquito from which he died a martyr's death to science, and in doing so he gave to the world a knowledge of how a fearful pestilence may be combatted and how humanity may be freed from anxiety and suffering from yellow fever.

Do you suppose that speeding through the air at a hundred miles an hour gives a greater thrill to the aviator than that which came to Sir William Herschel in 1781 when he realized that he had discovered the new planet, Uranus, the first of the planets to be discovered in historic times? "I have looked farther into space," he says exultantly, "than ever human did before me. I have observed stars of which the light takes two millions of years to travel to this globe."

Not long since Colonel Lindbergh, who has been called "the Columbus of the air," on his return trip from Central and South America stopped at Santo Domingo and visited the tomb of Christopher Columbus. During the long period between the discovery of America and the first aërial flight from New York to Paris, men impelled by the spirit of adventure have faced the perils of land, water and air seeking the unknown in inaccessible places of the earth. The courage displayed by some of these has been comparable to deeds of valor on the battle fields. The explanation for their sacrifices and privations is to be found in the intellectual hunger for knowledge and the instinctive longing of the human mind to learn more about the universe and the laws of its organization.

A short time ago Dr. Robert A. Millikan related to a distinguished group of scientists at the National Academy of Science in Washington how he discovered "cosmic rays" which pour upon the earth from out of space. His recital filled his audience with admiration for the persistency and ingenuity of America's greatest living scientist. He related his failure to obtain results on Pike's Peak. He then explained his experiments in Muir Lake on Mount Whitney in California, and then his trip to Bolivia in an effort to identify the illusive phenomena. He sent balloons with recording instruments into the heavens, some of which he was never able to find. He buried electroscopes far beneath the surface of mountainous lakes. The man who had previously succeeded in counting the number of molecules in a cubic centimeter of air had, by these remarkable methods, extended man's knowledge of space to new limits.

It is not possible for many men in any generation to duplicate the achievements of Galileo, Sir Isaac Newton, Sir William Herschel, Louis Pasteur or the other great scientists of the world; but it is possible for all of us to get satisfaction out of our pursuit of knowledge and it is not impossible to think of some you in the course of time making original contributions to the knowledge of the world. But the spirit of adventure in science is not confined to the research worker in search of new knowledge. All knowledge is new to him who is acquiring it for the first time. It is a dull intellect, indeed, that does not get a thrill of satisfaction out of its pursuit and conquest.

I like to meditate about this great adventure as thousands of students are enrolling in our schools, colleges and universities. I remind you that in these September days 4,000,-000 of our boys and girls resume their studies in the nation's high schools. Approximately 675,000 students will enter our colleges and universities. Twenty thousand of this total will enrol in institutions of higher learning in Oklahoma and more than 5,000 will seek knowledge in this university during the year. Think of what this means to the future of America and the world. The consequences are beyond the possibility of appraisal.

But I would not leave the impression that I think all this vast number of our youth will get a real thrill or find personal satisfaction in their intellectual endeavors. I know that there are many who are indifferent to their opportunities and largely unconscious of what is involved in this spiritual adventure. College life has its personal, moral and intellectual hazards. Many who are entering our institutions of higher learning today will come to grief in one way or another, and many others will find the difficulties too great to endure. Fortunate, indeed, is the student who is entering upon the quest of knowledge with a background of preparation and vital interest in the things of the spirit.

The story of Johnson's *Rasselas* is typical of the intellectual history of thousands of the youth of this country today. While this book is no longer read by many people, it has a real message for our times. Some of you may recall the story. Rasselas was the Prince of Abyssinia. He lived in a great palace in "Happy Valley." This Valley was completely surrounded by impassable mountains. The young Prince grew to manhood in this peaceful and pleasant environment but in time he became discontented and sought a knowledge of the larger world that lay beyond his mountain barriers.

Samuel Johnson tells us how Imlac, the man of learning, taught the Prince about the things of the world. "The first years of a man," says he, "must make provision for the last. He that never thinks never can be wise. Perpetual levity must end in ignorance; and intemperance, though it may fire the spirits for an hour, will make life short and miserable. Let us consider that youth is of no long duration, and that in maturer age, when the enchantments of fancy shall cease, and phantoms of delight dance no more about us, we shall have no comforts but the esteem of wise men, and the means of doing good. Let us, therefore, stop, while to stop is in our power; let us live as men who are some time to grow old, and to whom it will be the most dreadful of all evils not to count their past years but by follies, and to be reminded of their former luxuriance of health only by the maladies which riot has produced." I commend this philosophy of Imlac to you as worthy of your consideration today.

Rasselas finally made his escape from "Happy Valley" and with the knowledge imparted to him by his learned teacher he went forth in search of adventure. The larger world held many surprises, some disappointments and much knowledge for the young Prince.

The story of Rasselas epitomizes the life-history of youth in every age. The environment of childhood is one of restriction. It may be a "Happy Valley" filled with luxuries and comforts but the time comes in the life of every youth when the spirit of adventure predominates in his life and when he seeks the larger world of men and affairs.

The youth of today goes forth to appropriate two worlds— the spiritual and the mechanical. It is relatively easy for our young people to get a thrill out of the mechanical world of the present time. The automobile, the flying machine and the moving picture supply thrills that test the nerve and tax the emotions of the most daring of our youth. It is not quite as easy to experience similar emotions from the world of intellect and learning, but I remind you that the satisfactions of one may be not less real than the other.

There is no question that the pursuit of knowledge offers all the possibilities of adventure that come from high-speed machines and dramatic cinema productions. Remember that truth is often illusive. A geometrical principle, a law of nature, a fact of history, or the meaning of a poem may play hide and seek with you for hours, but to the true sportsman conquest is certain and the satisfaction resulting from the pursuit is usually proportional to the effort expended.

I commend to you the spiritual significance of the story

[59]

of Rasselas as you enter today a new world more complex than the world from which you came and whose intellectual challenge will test your resources of mind and heart.

I am wondering as you listen to me if the pursuit of knowledge has this appeal to you. The answer to this question must largely determine the amount of satisfaction you are to get out of your college contacts. The tragedies of college life result from the number of young men and young women who are intellectually dead to their environment. There are many of our young people who are coming up to college and university with no background of intellectual interest and no objective ahead as a goal of their efforts. *It is my duty to say, if any of you are here with a feeling that your interest lies wholly in social diversion or pursuit outside of laboratory and lecture halls, you should not waste your time in the fruitless pursuit of knowledge.* The intellectual life involves high adventure. He who seeks this life must pursue his way across trackless prairies and up the slopes of hazardous mountains. It penetrates to the depths of the fathomless oceans and stretches out into the spaces toward the distant stars. Your progress will not be easy or devoid of some discouragements but to the courageous and persistent truth-seeker the rewards are abundant.

A great American educator, in an interview quoted in a recent issue of one of our leading magazines, has said that "today, intellectually America is fast asleep! With all our boasted wealth, we are living educationally in a Dark Age." He places the blame for the situation upon our schools. "We have not made the child like school," says he, "nor have the schools made us an educated and cultured people. We have taken education like medicine, with a wry face and plenty of water. In brief, we have become unbalanced. We have grown materially but have lagged spiritually and intellectually. Football has superseded the classroom, *not* because there is anything wrong with football but because there *is* something wrong with the classroom. Instead of guiding our youth to understanding, we have been trying to stuff understanding down its throat by a process of forcible feeding, while professors stand by as policemen.

"We have been calling the college, or school, a preparatory course for life and utterly ignoring that it *is* life—that a boy's life is in progress as much when he comes to college as when he leaves it. We have been blaming the boy, the times, and outside influences for many failures that justly should be blamed to the school itself. We have let the classroom be ruled by tradition instead of by need, with the consequences that its methods have become antiquated.

"Give the average boy his choice between attending school or a circus, and he will choose the circus. The circus has set out to capture the boy's interest and has succeeded in doing it. The school has set out to do the identical thing and has failed. When I say circus, I mean any competitor of the classroom for youth's interest—the dance, the theater, football, society.

"The blame belongs on the school, and we should set about to remove it. If teaching methods are bad, we should find new ones. If textbooks are dry, we should rewrite them until they are interesting, or do away with them."

This perhaps is an overstatement of the defects of our educational system. Probably, this university president realized this himself, for he continues in a more optimistic vein to predict that "there is a new day coming, when schoolboys will find joy that thrills them in discovering and developing their own capacities, quite as much as in baseball or football; when college students will talk in dead earnest about economics, politics, chemistry, literature, biology and religion; when great monuments will be erected to teachers as creators of significant life."

This prophecy will be fulfilled when the intellectual atmosphere predominates in college life. I agree with Colonel William Wood, the scholarly historian of Canada, who says in one of his books that "a true intellectual life can only grow out of a national yearning for it. It cannot be bought; if it could the United States and Argentina might have an intellectual productiveness bearing some slight proportion to their trade returns. But it can be stunted, deformed and starved to death in stony places." Enthusiasm for learning and a real intellectual interest can come only from classrooms presided over by instructors with intellectual vision.

There can be no question that the intellectual life "can be stunted, deformed and starved" in a barren environment, but I do not believe that our educational institutions can be described in these terms. I am more inclined to agree with the appraisal of Dr. Frank Crane in one of his recent syndicated articles. "The school," says he, "is about the finest institution in the world. It is the greatest thing that social evolution has produced. What more ideal group could there be than a number of people, young or old, gathered together for the purpose of study!"

A remarkable front-page editorial in the educational section of the *Oklahoma City Times*, published during the past summer, calls the attention of the youth of the state to the fact that "education is great among the forces that have made men better than beasts, and brought them from savagery that held before the dawn of history. Knowledge has gained greater power as those who gleaned it learned to think. . . . . Never was a civilization in the recorded annals of time, but education held formidable place in its development. . . . . Nations rise and fall, but education endures within the minds of men, a cumulative heritage that those may share who will, and sharing, make the greater for the multitudes to follow." These are great generalizations that were directed to your attention and deserve your consideration as you enter upon your work today.

I sometimes wonder how much of the content of our courses of instruction conforms to the logical canons of truth. There is no question that there is much of error mixed with truth in the subject matter of instruction. *It is not only necessary that instructors possess the spirit of learning, but they must be intellectually honest and sincerely devoted to the pursuit of knowledge.* No teacher can impart enthusiasm for knowledge who does not possess these qualities.

In recent years much criticism has been directed at our colleges and universities. Blasting at the foundations of the temple of learning has become almost an American pastime. We are constantly being told that many college students are indifferent to their educational opportunities and that many instructors are poorly qualified for their tasks. We often hear these days that there is much lost motion in college organization and large funds are being dissipated in fruitless effort. We not infrequently hear that college students are going out poorly prepared and with no inclination to work industriously and efficiently at the tasks assigned them.

These criticisms have caused educators to resort to what Professor William Bennett Munro has called "quack-doctoring" in a well-considered article in *Harper's* for September (1928). After ridiculing these panaceas he concludes by saying: "There is no substitute and there never can be any substitute for *men* in the process of education—for earnest, enthusiastic, capable men in the faculty and in the student body. Given these, you have a great college, without them, all the newfangled methods will never avail an institution much. Nearly all the problems of collegiate education merge into two fundamental ones—*handpicking the student body and recruiting the faculty.* The college that does both these

[63]

things well is on the high road to ultimate distinction; and the one that relegates them to a secondary place in its program, while it goes philandering after mirages, is inexorably headed to the rear of the procession."

Professor Munro closes this article with a question that deserves to be answered in the affirmative by educators earnestly desirous of maintaining educational standards on a high plane of qualitative work. "Is it not time to rise and suggest the advisability of less quack-doctoring in the matter of our educational processes and more earnest concentration upon the vital issue of personnel?"

The challenge of college life today is to men and women, as teachers and students of high purpose, clear minds, strong wills and great hopes—to men and women who possess the spirit of sportsmanship in the quest of knowledge. If you can realize how small the intellectual world is in which you live, it will give you the spirit of humility. If you can visualize the scope of the world that lies today beyond your intellectual horizon, it will fire you with the zeal of conquest.

It is to this *sportsmanship in learning* that I direct your attention today. I hope now you are ready for the referee's signal and that you are eager to go. If you have courage, strength of mind and heart, honesty of purpose and persistency, you will win. In closing I commend to you Berton Braley's philosophy of success contained in the following poem:

"If you want a thing bad enough
  To go out and fight for it,
  Work day and night for it,
  Give up your time and your peace and your sleep for
[it,

  If only desire of it
  Makes you quite mad enough

Never to tire of it,
Makes you hold all other things tawdry and cheap for
[it,
If life seems all empty and useless without it
And all that you scheme and you dream is about it,
If gladly you'll sweat for it,
Fret for it,
Plan for it,
Lose all your terror of God or man for it,
If you'll simply go after that thing that you want,
With all your capacity,
Strength and sagacity,
Faith, hope and confidence, stern pertinacity,
If neither cold poverty, famished and gaunt,
Nor sickness nor pain
Of body and brain
Can turn you away from the thing that you want,
If dogged and grim you besiege and beset it,
      You'll get it!"

I hope that each of you wants an education "bad enough"
to "work day and night for it" and that

      "With all your capacity,
      Strength and sagacity,"

you may go forth to win. If you do, I can assure you

      "You'll get it!"

THE SPIRIT OF LEARNING IN A

MOTOR AGE[1]

CHAPTER SIX

THE assembling of a great student body at the beginning of an academic year is an occasion for reflection. It is, perhaps, much more than this. It is an occasion for serious introspection and the searching of hearts. Important questions naturally arise as we begin to think seriously about the days that are ahead of us. May I formulate some of these questions for you this morning? Why are you here? Are you seeking a deeper understanding and meaning of life and its values? Are you eager to acquire a broader intellectual perspective, to develop a wider range of experience, and to appropriate a definite and usable store of knowledge as a means of insuring to yourself a greater promise of security and a character that will stand the strain of temptation in the years that are to come? Have you come to the university with a sincere thirst for knowledge? Have you already made up your mind to pay the price in terms of sacrifice and sustained effort for the opportunities that you are to enjoy? The answers that you give to these questions in terms of conduct and general attitude will largely determine the measure of your success as college students.

1. Convocational address delivered at the opening of the thirty-eighth academic year on September 17, 1929.

The resources of the university are two kinds—material and human. About us here today are a number of buildings that house thousands of dollars worth of equipment that will be utilized for your instruction. Much has been expended in terms of money and effort in the beautification of this campus. When we speak of the university we usually think of these physical facilities, but I remind you that the real university is not a material thing of brick and stone and mortar. The thing that constitutes a real university is its human resources. In final analysis, it is this factor that determines the greatness of a university. These resources comprise officers, teachers and students.

About me on this platform this morning is the group of men and women that is giving to the university its reputation as an educational institution. The University of Oklahoma is absolutely dependent upon them for the good will of the people who support it and for its reputation for high scholastic standards throughout the world. You are dependent upon the character, the learning, the teaching ability and sincerity of purpose of this group of men and women for your intellectual advancement. Many of them have served this institution for many years; others, approximately thirty in number, have recently accepted appointments in the university. Between these two groups, there are more than two hundred men and women here who have served the university for a longer or a shorter period. I commend them to you as worthy of your confidence. I believe each of them to be competent to direct your intellectual endeavors.

It has become a habit with me to say at this annual convocation that this is the largest assembly of students that has ever enrolled at the beginning of an academic session. I repeat the statement this morning because it is true. In this growing state of ours, it is naturally to be expected that year after year our high schools will graduate an increasing number of students and that a corresponding increase in numbers will enrol in our institutions of higher learning. Students have enrolled in the university for this scholastic year from every section and, perhaps, from every county in Oklahoma. Many of you have come from other states and even from foreign countries. While hundreds of you are entering the university for the first time, there are great numbers in this audience who are resuming their studies after the summer vacation. To each and all of you I extend a cordial welcome to the university and express the hope and prayer that the days ahead may bring happiness, the consciousness of increasing strength of character and a realization of intellectual accomplishment.

In considering the human resources of a great university, we must take account, of course, of the fact that the component units are not equal in character or mental ability. You do not all come with equal preparation for your work. It goes without saying that not all of you will profit equally by your connection with the university. I fear some of you have not come for the primary purpose of acquiring a college education. It is too much to expect that the zeal for learning should be the consuming purpose of all of you but I hope that as time goes on these professors may be able to inspire, even in the most diffident among you, a real intellectual interest in the things of the spirit. There is no more deadening experience to which a college professor is subjected than that of undertaking to impart knowledge to a student who is not interested in the subject matter of instruction. I sometimes marvel at the power of resistance that some students have to the inculcation of learning. I regret that it is not possible to impart knowledge hypodermically, but no scientist has been able to find a method of bottling up the eternal verities and imparting them in the form of sugar-coated pills. Until this scientific discovery is made, I suppose our teachers will have to continue the old pedagogical methods of imparting knowledge in the old way. But the fact that the task is difficult in some cases should constitute a challenge to the teacher rather than a discouragement.

It is our earnest desire to create here an atmosphere of learning. I realize that the "temper of the times" is not conducive to straight thinking. We are living in a machine age with all attendant noises and distractions that result from the use of mechanical contrivances. In the past, learning has been associated with the quiet places—the cloister, the hermit's lodge and the mountain fastness.

As Abbé Ernest Dimnet says in his recent book entitled *The Art of Thinking*, "we cannot dissociate *solitude, freedom* and *leisure* from our concept of a life dedicated to thought: Spinoza in his one room where the carefully chosen monotony of his manual work acted on him as the monastic routine acted on a Benedictine scholar; Descartes leaving Paris for a quiet suburb of far-away Hague; Bossuet retreating like a hermit to the cabin at the end of his garden; Pasteur or Edison in their inviolate laboratories; learned monks in their convents; sages in the shady seclusion of a Massachusetts village; artists everlastingly trying to form colonies uniquely dedicated to disinterested work; all show us pictures of the kind of existence we imagine as naturally favourable to thought."

Those who have influenced the thought of the world most profoundly have sought at times places for meditation far away from the crowds and the distracting influence of city life. Socrates, Jesus, Savonarola, Immanuel Kant, Emerson and Gandhi are names that come to one's mind at the moment in this connection.

More than twenty-five years ago, William James, the greatest psychologist of his time, condemned the growing tendency of "overtension and jerkiness and breathlessness," to use his own phrase, that characterized American life. He regarded what he called "the absurd feelings of hurry" as detrimental to health and a handicap to mental efficiency. If James was impressed with the nervous tension of his day, I wonder what he would think of the situation at the present time. The mechanical forces about us today have greatly increased the consumption of nervous energy and there seems to be no place where one may go to find relaxation.

It is getting more and more difficult to find a place where one may freely exercise his intellectual powers. The motor car and the airplane now go everywhere. There are no places, no matter how remote from the haunts of man, where the hum of a motor may not be heard today. These great agencies of civilization are making one community out of all races and all nations but, at the same time, they are pre-empting the sacred precincts of learning of the quietude so essential to uninterrupted thought and meditation. One wonders what effect the enormous advance in mechanical invention with the changing habits produced by these inventions will have upon the spirit of learning.

We are hardly aware of the extent to which our lives are dominated by machines. We are in contact with mechanical forces from the time we awake in the morning until we retire at night. "The first thing I hear in the morning," says Stuart Chase in a recent article in *Harpers Magazine*, "is a machine—a patented alarm clock. In the bathroom I shave with one mechanism, and another showers me with water. Downstairs I look at an electric motor which blows petroleum into my furnace, a motor which runs the washing machine, and a motor which operates my refrigeration engine. Meanwhile an electric range is cooking my breakfast, and on the table slices of bread are being browned by a toaster which suddenly splits open when the correct shade of brown has been attained. Before I leave the house the whine of the vacuum cleaner is already in my ears.

"I go to the garage, start explosions in a six-cylinder engine, and pilot it past automatic signal lights to the station. There I resign myself to another man's operation of an enormous machine, fed by a third rail from a water turbine at Niagara Falls. Arrived at the metropolitan terminal I buy a package of cigarettes by depositing a coin in a machine which hands me matches and says, 'Thank you; it's toasted.' I enter my office building, and a machine shoots me vertically towards the roof. A sputter of typewriters greets me at my door."

We are profoundly indebted to the inventor and the scientist for making these agencies of civilization available to us. They have become an indispensable part of our lives; but as disease is always threatening to undermine health, social pathology always follows in the wake of progress. The blessings of mechanical invention are attended by consequences that are not altogether beneficial to society. Stuart Chase directs attention to this fact in the article from which I have quoted.

There are those today who contend that civilization will be destroyed by the very agencies that have determined its progress. These pessimists have expressed the belief that increased leisure made possible by machine production is resulting in habits that are undermining health and physical vigor. We know that security to life has greatly declined as the use of motor driven machinery has increased. We read in the daily newspapers of so many people being killed in motor accidents that we have almost ceased to be interested in these tragic occurrences. The automobile has certainly increased the insecurity of property and, as far as I am able to see, this will be further increased as commercial aviation develops. It seems that man's mechanical ingenuity has surpassed his social discernment. He is threatening the

[71]

stability of his social institutions by the mechanical contrivances he has developed for his convenience.

Paul Morand, in a recent article in one of our magazines, has expressed the thought that motor driven machinery has produced a new vice—the vice of a craze for speed. "A portion of the lure of speed," says he, "is that noble ambition to excel which has placed the Aryan race above the rest, but there is also a terrible excitement about speed which is beginning to intoxicate humanity. Observe the congestion in our cities, the desertion of the countryside. People can no longer bear either solitude or remaining in one place. Remaining in one place produces in us, if I dare say so, a fever for which speed is the remedy."

This writer touches on the real peril of a mechanical age to intellectual pursuits. The fact that people can no longer bear either solitude or remaining in one place is detrimental to those mental habits that are essential to intellectual accomplishment.

I wish every student present might read an article written by Deems Taylor and published in a recent issue of one of our magazines on "The Havoc Wrought by Professor Bell." He portrays in a most striking way the impossibility of doing "hard, clear, merciless thinking" (to use a phrase of H. G. Wells) in a modern home. He describes the demoralizing effect of the ringing of the doorbell and the tinkle of the telephone on one's efforts to think profoundly and continuously for a reasonable length of time on any subject of interest. The telephone is a great agency of civilization but it, also, plays a part in destroying that quiet solitude so much to be coveted by those who would commune with the muses.

John St. Loe Strachey, in his autobiography entitled *The Adventure of Living*, describes the Oxford environment of forty years ago as follows: "The happy undergraduate never has to catch a train, never has an editor or a printer waiting for him, never has an appointment which he cannot cut, never, in effect, has money to make." The high walls that still enclose the Oxford colleges, built centuries ago, were intended to secure a quiet environment to the scholar.

It is quite obvious that few students today in any part of the world are permitted to pursue their studies under the most favorable conditions. As a general thing, our educational institutions are located in the midst of feverish environments. The location of this university is no exception in this regard. While it does not require undue haste to catch a Santa Fe train in Norman, automobiles are rushing hither and thither, buses are clogging the thoroughfares and the motors of airplanes are frequently heard humming over our heads. Fortunately for you, even with these distractions, the University of Oklahoma is more favorably situated than many educational institutions. I think it exceedingly fortunate that this university is not located in a large city. I sometimes wonder how students ever develop the psychological attitude of real study in some of the institutions that have become an integral part of a great and growing city.

The task ahead of all of us interested in the promotion of real scholarship is to create an atmosphere around our educational institutions that will make the acquisition of knowledge relatively easy. The "no-car rule" at this university may contribute something to a wholesome collegiate environment but it is difficult, even here, to maintain a peaceful environment for those who seek favorable conditions for study.

We see evidence of high tension here as well as elsewhere. Students rush from class to class. They sit anxiously during lecture hours thinking of the limited time they will have at the close of the period to meet an appointment somewhere else. Students crowd their lives with a thousand and one engagements, most of them unnecessary and some of them actually detrimental to health and peace of mind. You cannot place the blame for this situation. It simply means that we have transferred the feverish anxieties and mental stresses of commercial life to the academic corridor and the inviting shades of the campus trees.

Emotional strain has profoundly influenced the literature of today. While a greater number of people are reading than ever before, the average amount of reading per individual has probably declined. Most of us read hastily and superficially. We have no time to read long articles in our magazines or books that are over sixty thousand words in length. The "three-decker" novels of Disraeli, Lord Lytton, George Meredith and others are no longer read. Occasionally, a gifted author, like Theodore Dreiser or John Cowper Powys, may write a two-volume novel and find a courageous firm that will take the risk of publishing it; but these are only exceptions that prove the rule that books must be short if their authors expect them to be read.

This is the day of outlines. We have outlines of literature, of art, of science, of philosophy, of religion, et cetera. The popularity of these outlines reflects the predominant characteristic of the age. We get satisfaction out of having a conversational knowledge of the literature of the past. These condensed outlines enable us to do this without the necessity of reading the voluminous volumes on which they are based.

Literature, itself, has felt the effect of this nervous tension. Henry Seidel Canby directs attention to this fact in his most recent book entitled *American Estimates*. He predicts that there will be no successors to the nature poets of the past. It is inconceivable, he thinks, that any modern poet can reproduce the memories of rural beauty as described in familiar poems of Wordsworth, Shelley and Keats. Dr. Canby expresses the belief that the rich beauty of Warwickshire, which suffused the poetry of Shakespeare, is forever lost to the poetry of today. The lament of Thomas Gray is, perhaps, as true of our age as his own:

"But not to one in this benighted age
    Is that diviner inspiration giv'n,
That burns in Shakespeare's or in Milton's page,
    The pomp and prodigality of Heav'n."

The modern poet can only communicate with nature through a machine. The poetic literature of today reflects the nervous, dynamic, feverish rhythm of the busy streets of our modern cities. This means that the art, the music and the literature of today will be quickly produced and quickly scrapped. It may produce wisdom but it gives no promise of providing rest and contentment. It is inevitable that books written in feverish haste should reveal grammatical errors and defective composition. Character delineation in the fiction of today is superficial and imperfect. Much of the serious literature of the times fails to penetrate the depths and the heights of the subject matter under consideration. It is not surprising, therefore, that most of the books we read today are forgotten tomorrow. I doubt if many of you can recall the titles and the authors of even the most popular books that you read a year ago.

This in itself may not be a misfortune. The thing to be regretted is that the mental distractions of today have left us without an inclination to read the masterpieces of the literature of the past. This is the reason that the literary reputations of the great writers have waned under the influence of the high tension and emotional strain of the present time. We still talk some of Shakespeare, Milton, Thackeray, Scott, Dickens, Carlyle, Ruskin, Washington Irving, J. Fenimore Cooper and Emerson but few read the works of these authors. Even those contributors to our philosophic and scientific literature who have most profoundly influenced the thought of the world, are rarely read even by the intellectuals of today. Plato's *Republic*, Bacon's *Novum Organum*, Kant's *Critique of Pure Reason*, Hegel's *Philosophy of History*, Carl Pierson's *Grammar of Science*, Darwin's *Origin of Species*, and Spencer's *First Principles* are conspicuous signposts on the intellectual highway of the centuries. But few people ever read these books today or even realize that they are the sources of the intellectualism of the present time. Probably not one of these authors, if he were living today, would have been able to produce the work on which his title to fame now rests. I am not saying that great books will not be written in the future, but I am speculating to the extent of saying that the writers of today and the immediate future will no more reproduce a volume like Kant's *Critique of Pure Reason* or Spencer's *First Principles* than our civilization will reproduce the cathedrals of Europe or the masterpieces of art that appeared during the Renaissance.

The conditions for clear thinking are not favorable. The mind is peopled with too many obsessions. The spirit of restlessness, anxiety and uncertainty crowds out productive ideas. The distractions about us make sustained attention very difficult. The favorable conditions to high thinking, out of which came the great scientific and philosophic literary productions of the past, have completely disappeared.

The spirit of learning implies the opportunity, as well as the power, to concentrate on the single object that engages one's attention. This means that the mind must be able to select the ideas to which it will attend at the moment and completely eliminate all images and impressions foreign to the object of thought. High and effective thinking involves concentration on related ideas of permanent value and the elimination of incongruous ideas. This has never been an easy thing to do but it is even more difficult when objective images contend for conscious recognition.

[76]

Every individual is constantly making choices. We not only choose to go to college or to stay at home, but we choose between the vocation of banking or the profession of law or medicine. Similarly, we are constantly choosing between ideas. It is not possible for us to do everything or to be everything. No one individual can be an athlete, a social lion, the best dressed man on the campus, a member of the glee club, a leader in debate, a student politician and a scholar at the same time. Every one who enters college must make choices between these conflicting interests. Upon the relative merits of these choices will depend one's happiness and success as a college student.

History has recorded some interesting examples of the choices that men have made. We are told in the book of Kings that the Lord appeared to Solomon in a dream by night and asked him what he most desired as he assumed his duties as sovereign of his people. His answer was: "Give thy servant an understanding heart." Contrast the choice of Solomon with that of Dionysius. We are told that Plato received an invitation from this powerful king of Syracuse to come and tell him how he could turn his kingdom into Utopia. Plato came and when he told Dionysius that it would be necessary for him to give up his kingship and become a philosopher, he declined. His displeasure at the suggestion was so great that he made Plato his slave and placed a ransom upon his head. This story illustrates the fact that many of us not only make wrong choices, but we are hostile to favorable decisions that lead to higher things. Few of us have the attitude of Solomon; many of us have the characteristics of Dionysius.

But, you stand today confronted with the problem of making numerous decisions. Some of them will affect your character, others will affect your intellectual life. Some of these decisions will not be easy for you to make, but they must be made and no one can make them for you.

I remind you that there is no royal road to learning. Character and wisdom come high but both are worth the price you pay in terms of long hours of labor and sacrifice to possess them.

I presume that this discussion seems rather academic to you, but as I have been speaking there has been in the background of my thinking a very practical situation. I wish, in conclusion, to make my thoughts as concrete as possible to you.

It is exceedingly difficult today for a college professor to impart knowledge to students. So much of a student's life in college is occupied with meaningless activity. The distractions about our institutions are so great as to make serious study exceedingly difficult. There are too many demands being made upon the student's time. The craze for social recognition, the ambition to participate in campus politics and the noisy environment about us are creating overtension and a spirit of anxiety that are serious obstacles to intellectual pursuits.

Conditions in our dormitories, fraternities, sororities and boarding houses are not always conducive to serious study. The frequent ringing of the doorbell and the telephone keeps students running about the building throughout the day and far into the night. Many students, particularly girls, are not getting sufficient sleep. The stress and strain are producing nervous disorders that are detrimental to health and perversive of intellectual accomplishment.

Houses occupied by students should be quiet places, at least during the evening hours. It should be understood that the evenings are to be given over to the preparation of the work of tomorrow. There should be a quiet hour on Sunday afternoon in all of our houses when every student should have an opportunity to relax completely. There should be no intrusion by outsiders on the privacy and peace of our campus homes during the hours assigned for solitude and rest.

The streets about the campus should be quiet at night. Students going and returning from the library, from conferences and from offices on the campus should respect the rights of those who are occupied by serious study or who are undertaking to sleep. I am certain we cannot develop the spirit of learning here at the university unless we all co-operate in creating conditions that make real study possible.

"Till this is done, our best pursuits are vain
To conquer truth, and unmixed knowledge gain."

THE HIGHER LEVELS OF LEARNING[1]

CHAPTER SEVEN

ON AN occasion like this, when faculties and students have assembled in great numbers to face the prospects and possibilities of a new college year, two questions naturally suggest themselves, whose answers challenge speculation and meditation. The first is:

What has a student a right to expect from his college?

The second question closely related to it is:

What has the student to give in terms of capacities, aptitudes, and loyalties?

I shall undertake today to answer in general terms the first question. The second question will be answered by each of you in your own way and in terms of intellectual accomplishment, fidelity of purpose, and general attitude of cheerful response to the policies and traditions of the university as the year progresses.

Dr. Le Baron Russell Briggs, for many years dean of the faculty of arts and sciences in Harvard University, once said on an occasion similar to this that "college life is the supreme privilege of youth," but he reminded his hearers that "the privilege of entering college admits to the privilege of deserving college; college life belongs to the great things, at once joyous and solemn, that are not to be entered into lightly." Professor Francis G. Peabody expressed this

1. Convocational address delivered at the opening of the thirty-ninth academic year on September 23, 1930.

thought most forcibly by saying that "when a youth enters college he passes from the sense of study as an obligation to the sense of study as an opportunity." I am hoping this morning that this is the spirit and attitude that you are assuming as you enter upon the year's work.

On the assumption that this is your attitude today, you are entitled to know what you may expect from your associations and experiences here. Perhaps I can best answer the inquiry that I have raised by telling you what a university is and why these educational institutions have come to occupy such an important place in our national life.

Cardinal John Henry Newman in his *Rise and Progress of Universities* defined a university as a "school of universal learning" and he proceeded to describe it as "the assemblage of strangers from all parts in one spot;—from all parts; else how will you find professors and from every department of knowledge? and in one spot; else how can there be any school at all? Accordingly, in its simple and rudimental form, it is a school of knowledge of every kind, consisting of teachers and learners from every quarter. Many things are requisite to complete and satisfy the idea embodied in this description; but such as this a university seems to be in its essence, a place for the communication and circulation of thought, by means of personal intercourse, through a wide extent of country." I like the phraseology of this description. A university is certainly an "assemblage of strangers from all parts in one spot." The students enrolled in this university, comprising more than 5,000, come from every county in Oklahoma, thirty-seven states of the United States, and several foreign countries. Most assuredly a university is "a place for the communication and circulation of thought, by means of personal intercourse, through a wide extent of country." Perhaps in this day of adult education we would enlarge somewhat on this definition; but essentially instruction is and always will be a matter of communicating thought by personal contact between student and teacher.

Cardinal Newman in this description was careful to tell us that a university is a place "for the communication and circulation of thought." Would it make any difference if we substituted the word knowledge for thought in this description? I think it would. Perhaps we would be more inclined to rephrase this sentence and say that a university is a place for the communication of knowledge and the circulation of thought.

Knowledge is communicated in a university. The vast resources of books and laboratories are designed to make knowledge accessible. Every educational institution worthy of the name has vast accumulations of these resources, which are made as accessible as possible for those who desire to use them. These men and women seated about me today and composing the several faculties of this university are charged with the responsibility of directing attention to particular sources of knowledge that are hidden away in musty volumes or concealed in the secret places of nature.

All knowledge is the product of experiences, experimentations, or logical conclusions. There is much current information that is accepted as knowledge that cannot stand these tests. There are, for example, many people above the average intelligence and education who believe that redheaded people always have quick tempers; that it is dangerous to eat fish and drink milk during the same meal; that tan shoes are cooler in summer than black; that lightning never strikes twice in the same place; that all Scotchmen are penurious and that no Englishman can readily see the point of a joke. In a world of enlightenment and universal education there are countless thousands of people who still "knock wood"; who think there is something sinister about the number thirteen, and who would not dare to begin a journey on Friday. I am not inclined to charge the teachers of the land with all the intellectual perversions of the human race, but there is much for them to do as long as there is as much loose thinking and as much superstition as there is still in the world.

The college student has a right to expect that his professor will impart knowledge that has been attested by the best possible methods of verification. Information imparted to students should, so far as possible, be purged of error. It has been inevitable that in the rapid accumulation of knowledge during the past century there should creep in a large element of error. The fact is, scientific truth does not come to us always in the purest form. It is often a long and difficult intellectual journey from the scientific hypothesis to the verified conclusion. I have no quarrel with the methods of the scientists. I believe in them. But I contend that the student is entitled to know the exact measure of truth—as far as it can be determined—that is contained in the information that is imparted to him. Professor Franklin H. Giddings in his latest book entitled *The Mighty Medicine* declares that "education that stops at sophistication is not merely vacuous, it is pernicious." His plea is for colleges to encourage "men and women to live wisely and sturdily on the experimental plane." There is no other escape from sophistication for those who seek verified knowledge for mere information.

But I fear we have come too much to assume that the communication of knowledge is all there is to education. We must never forget that the "circulation of thought" reflects the highest purposes of university life. The professor certainly is charged with the responsibility of imparting knowledge and developing skill in the use of the tools of knowledge. But this is not all of his task. It is the highest privilege of those who teach to inspire and to stimulate thinking. But no teacher can do the thinking for the student. It is the exalted and exclusive privilege of man to do his own thinking. The communication of our thoughts to others is an inviting privilege. But by no devices known to man can we compel others to accept our thoughts, nor can someone else compel us to substitute his thoughts for our own.

Education extends far beyond instruction in knowledge and the discipline of the mind. It must develop a sense of responsibility in the use of knowledge. *Civilization is confronted with but one greater peril than that of ignorance; that is the peril of vast accumulations of knowledge that is not consecrated to benevolent and beneficial ends.* It is one thing to make men wise and strong. It is quite another thing to make them good and great. It is one of the supreme functions of education to endow knowledge with the virtue of usefulness, and to motivate it with a high sense of social responsibility.

It is as important to train the will to respond to rational motives as it is to impart knowledge and develop skill in its use. Life is complex. Man is more than intellect. Will and action are of supreme importance and deserve careful attention in the educational process. Rational living is essential to happiness. We must recognize that life is constantly making paradoxical demands upon us, that every time we move we are making choices that are either wise or foolish. It is the high function of education to teach every individual to recognize these paradoxes as they occur and to act wisely with reference to them.

To state this situation in more concrete terms let me consider some of these paradoxes. In the physical life there is a constant conflict between physical relaxation and energized action. All of us are familiar with men and women who live listlessly, whose minds become inactive, and whose bodies become flabby because of failure to exercise the muscles of the body in useful endeavor. There is no challenge in life to spur them on to energetic endeavor. Mental and physical inertia cannot be overcome. Mental and physical relaxation cause degeneration of muscular and intellectual faculties. On the other hand, there are those who are overenergized. They live at high tension. They often exhaust their mental and physical energies in misdirected effort. Sometimes their energies are utilized in profitable pursuits. Most of these people are inspired by high motives. But too often a nervous breakdown is the price they pay for their good deeds. Happy is the man or woman who guides a course between these undesirable extremes.

In the intellectual life we are constantly confronted with the paradox of giving attention to the things that are essential and ignoring the things that are unessential. Discrimination is always at war with assimilation in the processes of learning. This is illustrated every day in the lecture rooms of our colleges and universities. We see students taking copious notes without discriminating between the significant and the casual. The exposition of a principle and the illustration by which it is illuminated are equally significant. I observed a number of people this summer in Europe who were rushing from place to place with notebooks and pencils in their hands. Most of these people were so busy writing down what their guides were saying that they failed to see the pictures on the walls or the statues about them in the art galleries.

In the moral life paradoxes repeatedly occur. Procrastination is constantly in conflict with prompt decision. There are some of us who procrastinate so long that we never get anything done. There are others who act so promptly upon every impulse that most of their decisions are wrong. It is perhaps better to act on impulses than not to act at all; but education has no higher function than to train men and women to recognize this moral paradox and to make deliberation habitual, yet to decide promptly when sufficient evidence is at hand.

President Henry Churchill King, to whom I am indebted for this approach to life, reminds us also that "quietism wars with enthusiasm—the mood of the East with the mood of the West—and yet we can spare neither." But, there are those who carry the virtue of "quietism," to use Dr. King's word, to the extreme of reticence and timidity. On the other hand, there are those whose enthusiasm is so bounteous as to effervesce in the thin air of unreality. This paradox is closely akin to the overemotionalized individual who exhausts his mental energy in false sentiments. It is, as every psychologist knows, the restrained emotions that invigorate and vitalize, as well as the indulgent emotions that exhaust, that strain, and drain the mental life of its most subtle reserves.

Even in religion there is the paradox between rationalism and mysticism. There are those that are so rationalistic as to eliminate the realm of faith from their thinking. On the other hand, there are those who are so mystical that their religion is devoid of reason and valid truth. The sane religious individual must take account of verifiable knowledge while recognizing that there is much of reality that lies in the realm of faith and beyond the reaches of the finite.

The recognition of the golden mean between these paradoxical extremes is essential to rational living. As Aristotle pointed out in his *Ethics*, courage lies somewhere between rashness and cowardice; liberality between prodigality and stinginess; temperateness between continence and gluttony; magnanimity between boasting and self-disparagement; friendliness between false praise and cynicism; modesty between bashfulness and imprudence; and truthfulness between falsehood and exaggeration.

The university has no higher function than that of training men and women to live rationally on the highest levels of intelligence. While this objective is less tangible than formal instruction, it is the underlying philosophy of every college curriculum. The by-products of academic, technical and professional training should be a wholesome attitude toward life and greater ability to live rationally.

Candor compels me to say that it is not always easy to realize this ultimate objective under existing programs of education. The elective system of courses that was first introduced into the curricula of our colleges and universities some seventy-five years ago in response to the recognition of the varied aptitudes of students, the rapid increase in the body of knowledge, and the demand for more specialized training to meet the needs of our complex civilization has produced consequences that could not be foreseen at the time. I am sure the early advocates of the elective system, were they alive today, would be surprised to see that chaos has been wrought by the innovation that they introduced into the educational system. It could not be foreseen, of course, to what extremes the elective system would go in completely displacing classical learning and in fractionalizing the contents of the curricula. It is not easy for the student to get a proper perspective of knowledge when closely related subject matter is taught in unrelated departments. In our efforts to meet the needs of students of diverse aptitudes and to make the learning task as easy as possible, we have dissociated intellectual discipline from habits of study and largely relieved the minds of youth from the exercise of critical judgments. It is perfectly natural for us to want to make the road to learning as easy as possible, but in an effort to improve the highway of learning we have provided so many detours that the student has found it difficult to find his way back to the broad highway that leads to intellectual accomplishment.

In the attainment of the higher levels of learning we

[87]

should utilize all the resources at our command. Preparation for effective living today involves much more than appropriating the content of books and acquiring the discipline that comes from rigid laboratory measurements. Without disparaging the more formal aspects of learning, I am inclined to believe that the contacts in college and university communities with men and women of high intellectual attainments, attractive personalities, and varied experiences are perhaps the greatest privilege of youth in their efforts to equip themselves for appropriating the best that our complex civilization offers.

We must not forget that a college community differs essentially and vitally from all other types of communities composing our national life. We should take pride in this fact and utilize every effort to make it distinctive. It is a place where personality should count for the most, where friendships may be formed without the alloy of selfishness, and where the trivialities of the outside world may be ignored. For this reason, everything that is done in a university community should reflect good taste and conform to sound social traditions.

There is a tendency these days to ridicule social conventions and to disparage the old accepted virtues. I would remind you that our social conventions have come down to us after centuries of experimentation. Out of the trial-and-error method men have learned what experiences produce happiness and promote progress, and what forms of conduct result in misery and retardation. The virtues of honesty, truthfulness, courage, and justice have found a place in every ethical system of the world. We should cultivate them and reflect them in our social relations with each other.

What then has a student a right to expect of his college? First of all, he has a right to expect to be taught the eternal truth by men and women of conviction and knowledge. In the second place, he may expect to acquire the habit of thinking on a high plane. He should expect his college to help purge his mind of misinformation and free his thoughts from superstition. In the third place, he has a right to expect the university to impart a sense of responsibility in the use of knowledge. He has a right to expect that the university will help to direct the knowledge that he has acquired to beneficial ends.

Finally, he has a right to expect that out of his contacts and experiences here, he will be better able to live sanely and profitably in all the relations of life. A sound philosophy of life should be one of the direct products of every man's educational experience. No man can rightfully claim to be educated whose conduct is not anchored in convictions that have been arrived at through thoughtful consideration of their consequences.

This is what the university has to offer. Are you prepared in mind and heart to receive these gifts? This is the question I leave with you on this opening day of the new college year.

CHANGING ATTITUDES TOWARD LEARNING[1]

CHAPTER EIGHT

THIS convocation marks the formal opening of the fortieth annual session of the university. Year after year, throughout the history of the university, faculty and students have assembled about this time and considered together the work and the problems of the new year. No two college years are ever exactly alike. A constantly changing student body, as well as rapidly changing world conditions, make each year unique in the life of an institution of higher learning. Today is not like yesterday, and tomorrow will be different from today. This we know from experience. The world in which we live is characterized by change, and we experience all the influences incidental to the silent forces that are at work about us.

Think for a moment of some of the important events that have occurred since we last assembled in this place for our great commencement exercises in June. The President of the United States has proposed a moratorium to the nations of Europe; Germany has passed through a serious financial crisis; and more recently the labor government in England has been dissolved and a coalition government has been formed in an effort to prevent a political upheaval. Only a

1. Convocational address delivered at the opening of the fortieth academic year on September 22, 1931.

short time ago, the press of the world reported the renewal of the conflict between church and state in Italy; and Spain, after overthrowing her monarchy, has established a republican form of government. While these events were taking place abroad, our own state and national governments have been engaged in desperate efforts to solve the problems of unemployment, crime prevention, the conservation of our mineral resources, and the stabilization of the price structure.

While political history of the greatest significance was being made throughout the world, men of courage and daring were breaking records through their exploits in the air. Auguste Piccard, a Swiss scientist, soared in a balloon to an altitude of 52,000 feet, breaking the world's record. Harold Gatty and Wiley Post, the latter an Oklahoman, circumnavigated the globe in an airplane. They traveled 15,474 miles in eight days, fifteen hours, and fifteen minutes. The day after these daring aviators left New York, Otto Hillig and Holger Hoiriis took off from Harbor Grace, Newfoundland, and landed in the late afternoon of the following day at Bremen. A few days later Russel Broderson and John Polando flew from New York to Constantinople and set a new nonstop distance record by flying over 5,000 miles in forty-nine hours. One morning in July Frank Hawks, who was the pilot for Will Rogers when he came to the university last spring, ate breakfast in London, flew to Rome for his lunch, and was back in London for an early evening dinner. The leisurely flight of Colonel and Mrs. Lindbergh over an uncharted route in the far North from New York to Tokio is of recent occurrence.

These events merely illustrate the nature and importance of daily happenings in the dynamic world in which we live. History is being made every day. Traditions are being discarded and precedents are being broken on every hand.

The spirit of adventure is in the air. Life is being lived dangerously on new levels of experience.

Some of the things that have happened during the past summer will influence world affairs for all time to come. Educational institutions cannot ignore the temper of the times. Our thinking about life and destiny is being permanently altered. Our attitudes toward many economic, social, political, and moral questions are being profoundly modified by the cross-currents that chill and thrill us day after day.

There is not a subject of instruction that can be taught in exactly the same way as it was taught last year. The currents of thought and the spirit of adventure that are so much in evidence must penetrate every classroom. It is true that acids will still react on soluble salts in test tubes as they have always reacted. The smears upon microscopic plates will look as they have in the past. Mathematical deductions will lead to the same conclusions. But all of these facts have new meanings in the light of world events about us. The fact that Colonel and Mrs. Lindbergh flew to Tokio gives new meaning to the history of human relations. The historic fact that Ramsey MacDonald placed country above party and became the head of a new coalition cabinet in England makes it necessary for college professors to revise their repertoire of Scotch jokes to enliven classroom instruction.

The conditions of life about us have greatly changed the attitudes of freshmen. Until very recent times the transition from school to college was looked upon as an adventure. Every freshman entered college with a sense of timidity and genuine anxiety. I recall the words of President Albert Parker Fitch of Andover Theological Seminary in describing the state of mind of the freshman in 1914:

"For that year [the freshman]," says Dr. Fitch, "is always and everywhere a high adventure. It is compounded of delightful if terrifying uncertainties. It is the exploration, big with fate, which each awakening youth makes into the real world of his fellow human beings, into the real convictions, desires, and powers of his own soul. There still comes once, to every boy, even in our safe and comfortable and commonplace world, a morning when the mystery and the thrill of the Unknown lay hold upon him; when the call of the undiscovered country is in his ears; when he knows that, at last, he is free to walk an untrodden path and to do and be what no one else has ever done or been before. That is the morning of the day when college opens, and he, once a schoolboy, now an undergraduate, stands, his own master, at his dormitory door."

This description seems far-fetched and remote to us today. The "safe and comfortable and commonplace world," to which Dr. Fitch referred, no longer exists. The freshman does not feel today as he enters college that he is "to walk an untrodden path." While he is fully aware that he is an undergraduate, this does not cause him to have an inferiority complex. The average freshman has an assurance that the freshman of other days did not possess. Sometimes this assurance borders on sophistication, but perhaps even this state of mind is to be preferred to one of depreciation and uncertainty.

In my younger days as a college president one of the most serious problems that confronted the faculty at this season of the year was that of ministering to homesick students. In those days, the first weeks of most college students were characterized by frequent spells of homesickness. I became an expert diagnostician of this malady. The disease took many forms and manifested itself in many ways. But I came to know its various symptoms and, in time, I acquired great resourcefulness in treating the malady. Homesickness, however, like typhoid and smallpox, is on the decrease. I do not attribute this fact to a lack of affection for parents or attachment for home life. The conditions of life about us have widened the experiences of youth and developed a spirit of independence that was not possible in the past.

This does not mean, however, that there are not anxieties incident to entering upon a college career. These anxieties, of course, change from year to year. I am sure that at this time the economic depression is giving deep concern to hundreds of you. I have never known so many students in any one year who needed financial assistance to enable them to enter college. Throughout the summer hundreds of students have sought loans or opportunities to earn part of their expenses. It has been impossible for the university to extend assistance to all worthy students who have applied to us for help, but the earnest efforts that countless thousands of the youth of the land are making to acquire a college education demonstrate the ambitions and aspirations of our young people and reveal a willingness to make sacrifices to accomplish their ambitions that is truly commendable.

Times like these demonstrate the value of a college education. Millions of men are out of work; but, generally speaking, the marginal man is always the first to suffer in vocational competition when periods of industrial and financial adjustments come. In other words, the ignorant and the untrained are the first to experience the adverse effects of hard times. While it is true that the extent of this depression has brought hardships to countless thousands that do not belong to the marginal group of employees, it is, nevertheless, a fact that the marginal man has been the first to suffer and he will be the last to obtain relief. This fact not only demonstrates the value of a college education, but it brings home to every boy and girl the need for preparation for vocational and avocational life.

I remind you, also, that every educational institution in

the country is experiencing the hardships that have come to individuals and corporate groups as a result of the economic depression. All of our colleges and universities will be compelled to operate this year on a reduced budget. The University of Oklahoma and state-supported institutions everywhere have been compelled to curtail activities or to reduce their administrative and teaching forces. Some have been forced to do both. This situation has created serious problems of administration. A number of our educational institutions have undertaken far-reaching experiments in an effort to find a way out of their difficulties. It is not easy at the moment to predict what will be the ultimate effects of our present economic situation upon our educational institutions.

But there are compensations connected with every situation of this kind. Human nature is such that mankind can endure just so much prosperity for a limited time. It was inevitable that the fat years following the World War must end sometime. We were rapidly losing the sense of relative values. Many had come to believe that speculation could be substituted for thrift, that sophistry could replace clear thinking, and that spiritual values were no longer essential to human happiness.

It is regrettable that it often takes adversity to restore reason and sober-mindedness to a people. In the mad rush of the last decade we forgot that the greatest perils to nations and civilizations come in times of prosperity rather than in times of adversity. History teaches that the seed of destruction in national life is usually sown in times of greatest prosperity. The fall of Assyria, Babylonia, Greece, and Rome all bear witness to this fact. The Periclean Age in Greece was followed by the Peloponnesian War, which marked the end of Athenian supremacy. The Augustan Age in Rome was followed by a steady decline in political leadership until an alien people marched through the

[95]

mountain passes to the fair plains of Italy and occupied the capital of the Caesars. Years of adversity seem to follow periods of prosperity as night follows the day. Natural law seems to underlie the one almost as surely as it does the other. Both play their part in determining life and destiny.

What are the lessons that we should learn from the adversity of our times? This seems to be an appropriate question for us to raise and attempt to answer. It was not easy to maintain a spirit of learning during the recent period of prosperity. The years following the World War were hard ones for educators everywhere. Life could be lived so freely that learning seemed superfluous. The exacting demands of scholarship were alien to the temper of an easy age. Money was plentiful and it could buy the comforts of life. Why should anyone spend laborious years in the study of philosophy, literature, history, science, and art? Successful business men, who measured life in terms of dollars, were telling us that a college education was not essential to success. In times of widespread prosperity, such preachments are hard to refute. But, I dare say, there are few men today who would attempt to disparage the value of a college education. While, of course, the intellectual is sharing the hardships incident to our general economic situation, he is mentally better able to endure the strain, and do it philosophically, than any other type of our citizenship.

I have been interested in the numerous proposals that have been advanced for the relief of economic distress. Some of our most forward looking statesmen have proposed that the way to prosperity lies through vast governmental expenditures for public projects of various kinds. It has been proposed that large sums be expended on public highways. Congress has already entered upon a vast public building program in Washington. Improvement of our waterways and an increase in our water-power resources have been suggested.

Strange as it may seem, no man in public life has proposed vast expenditures on our cultural resources as an aid to the restoration of prosperity. I have no disposition to disparage governmental expenditures for public works as a means of solving the unemployment problem that is so serious today. On the other hand, I think that this movement should be encouraged; however, I am frank to say that any program involving public expenditures that does not include our cultural resources is inadequate and shortsighted. I was gratified to read in a recent issue of the *New York Times* (Sunday, September 6, 1931) a statement by Carl E. Grunsky of San Francisco, President of the American Engineering Council and recently appointed by President Hoover a member of the organization for unemployment relief headed by Walter S. Gifford, advocating this very policy. He says:

"The nation's spiritual and cultural advancement are of greater importance than provision for material well-being. Expenditures of public funds for such purposes comparable with those for the safeguarding of life and property, for the protection of health and for facilitating the exchange of products would not be unreasonable; but there is fear of the tax burden.

"Under a well-balanced program the nation would get vastly more scientific research and educational opportunity. Art should be encouraged by the erection of monuments, the establishment of museums, art galleries, conservatories of music and opera houses with maintenance of opera companies in all centers of population. Expenditures for these purposes would contribute to the spiritual uplift of the people and to the progress of civilization.

"Provision for outdoor recreation should be made throughout the land on a scale never yet approached.

Lands should be reserved and acquired so that those who get into the open may find suitable places to picnic and to camp. During periods of declining prices there should be also a speeding up of public works on a sane program. Recourse to pick and shovel, instead of to modern appliances, is but a trifle above giving a dole with its encouragement of idleness and of return to primitive conditions."

A five-day week and a shorter working day have been suggested as one of the means of solving the unemployment problem. Unless there is a wider range of human wants, there seems to be no other way out of our existing difficulties. This redivision of vocational opportunity will, of course, enlarge the avocational, cultural, and recreational opportunities for everyone; but for society to enlarge vocational opportunities without, at the same time, providing for the wisest possible utilization of the free time and energies of the people would merely be shifting the problem from one sphere of activity to another. It seems, therefore, that it is highly important for all of us to see this problem in all its relations. In other words, it is equally as important to provide adequate cultural and recreational opportunities as it is to solve the problems of unemployment by reducing the labor load.

One of our great daily papers said editorially last summer that "there is one debt for which no moratorium can with safety be declared. That is the eternal debt of maturity to childhood and youth—education.

"After health and physical safety it is the first obligation of the state. Not only should the schools now be kept going at their best, but children and youth who are normally drawn into industry at a younger age should be encouraged to continue their schooling rather than seek employment in competition with older persons, who cannot so readily adapt themselves to changed conditions. This may often mean parental sacrifice, but it is the best investment that can be made when it is at all possible."

Little has been said about the aid that our schools and colleges can render in helping to solve the unemployment problem. There is no question that the schools can assist in this enterprise. Students should not only be encouraged at this time to enter college for their own benefit, but as a means of withdrawing hundreds of them from competition with mature men who have families to support.

I am hoping that you have entered, or re-entered, college today with the full realization of the conditions of life about you. It is possible for each of us to feel a deep sense of our pressing obligations without sacrificing happiness or contentment. The time has come for us to think soberly and seriously about life and its possibilities. If there ever was a time to practice plain living and high thinking, it is now. The student who lives extravagantly this year is unworthy of college opportunities. Student groups of every kind should encourage and practice economy. The closest possible scrutiny will be exercised on the part of university authorities in an effort to impress students with the importance of living simply and sanely.

But there is a much higher obligation resting upon each of you than the mere practice of economy. I refer to the obligation of making the best possible use of your opportunities. I admit this sounds trite, but it is a truism that requires emphasis today. This university is no place for a loafer. Indifference to the acquisition of knowledge and its values is a deadly sin here. Every one of you will be expected to report to classes promptly, to attend regularly, to sustain an attentive attitude while in classes, and to respond cheerfully to the demands made upon you by your instructors.

That is not all. You will be expected to assume the right attitude toward knowledge. All that any professor can do

[99]

is to expose you to knowledge. It is your duty to assimilate it. *The higher ethics of college life involve responsive attitudes toward truth.* No man can live at the higher intellectual levels unless he has an adequate perspective of all knowledge. An adequate understanding of some sphere of knowledge is essential to rational living.

From time to time during your college course you should attempt to make an evaluation of the knowledge you have acquired. I read of a student recently who attempted to do this. He set down a list of things he had learned. Some of them were:

How to sleep in a chair while sitting erect.

How to turn off an alarm clock without waking up.

How to read a book by scanning the first sentence of every paragraph.

That the ancient Greeks were smart people.

That psychology is more interesting in novels than textbooks.

That Columbus didn't discover America.

That it is bad to *always* split your infinitives.

We are inclined to laugh at this student's intellectual accomplishments. But, certainly, he had learned something. It is quite an art to sleep while sitting erect in a chair. He certainly did not list all the things he had learned. It is quite apparent that this student had acquired the spirit of fortitude and patience while sitting in class suffering at times from insomnia. I remind you, also, that this youth had learned that an infinitive could be split. There are still some people who are entirely ignorant of this fact!

A university campus is a place where every man and woman should seek the maximum opportunity to enrich his or her life by the greatest possible number of valuable experiences. H. G. Wells in his *First and Last Things* declares that it is an essential duty of every man to utilize his experiences to this end. "The general duties of a man," says he, "his existence being secured, is to educate, and chiefly to educate and develop himself. It is his duty to live, to make all he can out of himself and life, to get full of experience, to make himself fine and perceiving and expressive, to render his experience and perceptions honestly and helpfully to others." There is no better place in all the world to accomplish these ends than in a university.

I invite each of you to share fully in the life that is lived on this campus. Seek the best that the institution offers to you. Live daily in the consciousness of what is going on in the great world that lies beyond our campus. Remember that the spirit of adventure is in the air. Translate this experience into your own conduct by adventuring far into the unknown land of knowledge. Adapt your attitudes toward learning to the changing world situation.

I think I can do no better than to recall, in conclusion, the familiar words of Solomon:

Get wisdom, get understanding: forget not: neither decline from the words of my mouth.

Forsake her not, and she shall preserve thee: love her, and she shall keep thee.

Wisdom is the principal thing; therefore get wisdom: and with all thy getting get understanding.

Exalt her, and she shall promote thee: she shall bring thee to honor, when thou dost embrace her.

She shall give to thine head an ornament of grace: a crown of glory shall she deliver to thee.

Hear, O my son, and receive my sayings; and the years of thy life shall be many.

I have taught thee in the way of wisdom; I have led thee in right paths.

When thou goest, thy steps shall not be straightened; and when thou runnest, thou shalt not stumble.

Take fast hold of instruction; let her not go: keep her; for she is thy life.

This is sound advice from a high source. A great promise is held out to those who utilize instruction for the purpose of acquiring knowledge and wisdom, but the faith of thousands has been strengthened by seeing this promise to youth fulfilled time and time again. I commend the admonition of the wise man of old to you today with the utmost confidence that if you heed it, *thy steps shall not be straightened; and when thou runnest, thou shalt not stumble.*

DISCOVERY AND LEARNING[1]

CHAPTER NINE

THE EXERCISES of this hour mark the opening of the forty-first annual session of the University of Oklahoma. Education at all levels, from the elementary school to the university, has received serious consideration at the hands of the people of this state. The University of Oklahoma was brought into existence through an act of the Territorial Legislature of Oklahoma in 1890, and the first academic session began in the fall of 1892. During this entire time reasonable financial support has been provided and thousands of students have sought the educational advantages offered here. While forty years is a relatively short period of time as we measure the history of universities in this country and in Europe, appraised in terms of accomplishment the period has been a significant one.

Faculty members and students have assembled about this time each year as the work of a new session has begun. It happens that no two years of college life are ever exactly alike. New conditions and new problems arise from time to time that change the outlook and create a new situation for every educational institution. Certainly, we are beginning this college year with new problems confronting us. The years of economic and financial distress have seriously affected educational institutions everywhere. The Univer-

1. Convocational address delivered at the opening of the forty-first academic year on September 20, 1932.

sity of Oklahoma, like all other agencies of human society, is seriously affected by these conditions. The institution has been compelled to adopt a policy of retrenchment—retrenchment that has cut deep into the resources of the institution. But I wish to assure you that while strict economy will need to be practiced this year, every possible effort will be made to maintain the standards of instruction that have prevailed in the past.

I am fully aware that many of you are coming to college with limited resources. To some of you this will mean privation; to others, extreme hardship. But I think you are wise in coming to college this year. Fortunately for you, there has not been a time in a generation when you could attend school as economically as you can today. It is desirable for you to enter college this year because opportunities for employment are very limited; and with the thousands of men and women, who are the sole support of families, out of employment, it is better for our country that you avoid vocational competition and prepare for the better days that are ahead.

But while this is an anxious time, I do not believe that we should yield to discouragement or despair. The history of the past should supply us with some encouragement for the future. The university has had difficulties in other years. It passed through the trying period of the World War. These were years of uncertainty and difficulty. Even more serious difficulties have confronted the university from time to time, but the institution has weathered every storm and passed through every crisis in its continued march of progress. Let us hope that it will come through the present economic depression in the same way.

I remind you that there has never been a time since the university opened its doors that there were not students enrolled who were poor in purse but ambitious to secure an education. Many of these today are among the state's most useful citizens. Some of them have won distinction in almost every field of human endeavor. What they have done, you can do. While the number of you who are confronted with financial difficulties today is undoubtedly far greater than the number in any preceding year, your individual difficulties are not greater than those of others who have preceded you in the quest for an education.

It is not my intention this morning to dwell upon these problems. I prefer to direct your thoughts in other channels. The subject of my discussion was suggested by an advertisement that apeared recently in the *Saturday Review of Literature* in which a young man sought employment. He recommended himself in the following words:

"Young intellectual (?) unblighted by civilization, naturally sensitive, responsive (depending on stimulus), freed of inhibition, *et al.*, and highly articulate, *interested in being discovered.*"

This advertisement impressed me as being rather unusual. After meditating over the phraseology of this description, I began to speculate as to how many of our young people might be catalogued in these terms. It occurred to me that perhaps this young man, after all, might not be so very different from many other young men and women, particularly those who are enrolled in our colleges and universities.

I do not know, however, to what extent the average college student is "unblighted by civilization" or to what degree he is "highly articulate" because I am not sure that I know what these phrases mean; but I am sure that most college students are responsive to stimuli (not always to the stimulus of learning) and that they are rather free (perhaps too free) of inhibitions. But it is reasonable to presume that every young intellectual is interested in being discovered and that this is the essential reason for his coming to college.

[105]

It is important, both for student and teacher, to think of learning as a means of discovery. Education, perhaps, is too much thought of today merely in terms of the acquisition of knowledge which the student is taught to analyze, to criticize, and to apply. We do not think enough about learning as a measure of intelligence or a gauge to the quality of thinking. After all, the qualities of mind and heart that the student manifests toward his work and the capacities that he reveals for accomplishment are more important than the quantity of knowledge acquired. The end of learning is scholarly habits, by which I mean ability to work with intensity, with patience, with thoroughness, and with eagerness. Rightly conceived, learning should reveal the qualities of integrity, the spirit of self-detachment, and an attitude of self-abnegation. These qualities should become the conscious possession and the attitude of mind of every student as he discovers his innate talents through the learning process.

"Know thyself," says Socrates. Ignorance of self is life's greatest handicap. Philosophers through the ages have been concerned with the problem of explaining the process by which man discovers himself by knowing the world about him. The modern psychologists, irrespective of the school to which they adhere, have been primarily concerned with the methods of exploring the human mind. Intellectuals in all ages have sought a method, a technique, that would enable them to measure their own mental, physical, moral, and spiritual endowments. "Men and women," says Albert Edward Wiggam, "never needed psychology so much as they need it today. Young men and women need it in order to measure their own mental traits and capacities with a view to choosing their careers early and wisely." But this is only one of the reasons why they need it. They need it as a means of determining consciously the conditions of growth and their capacities for happiness and influence.

"So much of our lives," says Will Durant, "is meaningless, a self-cancelling vacillation and futility; we strive with the chaos about us and within; but we would believe all the while that there is something vital and significant in us, could we but decipher our own souls." These words lay bare the secret tragedies in many lives. So much of our thinking is meaningless. There is so much of futility in our acts; while, at the same time, we are conscious "that there is so much that is vital and significant in us" which we do not seem to be able to turn to account. The learning process fostered in college should help us to know ourselves and to decipher the vital and significant things in our lives.

Socrates is reported, on one occasion, to have given an exposition of the doctrine that we should know ourselves. Xenophon in his *Memoirs* records a conversation between the philosopher and a rather conceited and sophisticated young man by the name of Euthydemus, whom he was attempting to impress with this truth. Socrates used a striking analogy in his argument with this youth. He said:

"But for a man to know himself well, it is not enough for him to know his own name: for a man that buys a horse, cannot be certain that he knows what he is, before he has ridden him, to see whether he is quiet or restiff; whether he be meddlesome or dull, whether he be fleet or heavy; in short before he has made trial of all that is good or bad in him; in like manner, a man cannot say that he knows himself, before he has tried what he is fit for, and what he is able to do. . . . . For he who knows himself, knows likewise what is good for himself. He sees what he is able to do, and not able to do. By applying himself to things that he can do, he gets his bread with pleasure, and is happy; and by not attempting to do the things he cannot do, he avoids the danger of falling into errors, and of seeing himself miserable."

This striking plea of Socrates for discovery through learning is valid today. There is but one way to evaluate experiences, and that is through knowledge that gives exercise to all the faculties of the mind.

The essential reason for attending college is for the purpose of enlarging human experience under conditions where every mental and physical activity can be measured in terms of its consequences. There is no other place where the range of human experience is so wide or so varied. The home environment from which you have come is, as it should be, a rather restricted environment. While it is not so restricted as it once was, by the very nature of things it is and always will be a limited environment. There is nothing so disastrous to a growing child as multiplying experiences faster than mental and physical growth warrant. Parents have no greater responsibility than that of restricting the child's activities to its ability to assimilate the enlarging environment in which it lives. The environment into which young people go after their college days are over will, also, be a restricted environment no matter under what conditions they live or work. Business and professional life, perhaps, is not quite so restricted today as in the past, for a conscious effort has been made by community agencies to enlarge the interests and activities of the busy man with exacting duties and responsibilities. But, at best and by necessity, there is much of restriction in the lives of most mature people. University life has the advantage over the home environment and the environment of business and professional life in giving a wider range to individual interests. This has not always been true. Throughout the early history of higher education in this country, the college environment was in some respects more restricted than the early home environment. There was little place for social activities. There were few recreational opportunities, and athletics were unimportant and generally discouraged. But for the last half century this picture has been rapidly changing. Social and recreational activities have multiplied rapidly until today student life comprehends a range of interests to be found nowhere else in our social life. The fact is that our educational institutions have deliberately stimulated many of these activities as a means of vitalizing and intensifying the interests of students in order to test out human aptitudes and evaluate capacities and limitations.

While the range of human experience that this environment stimulates is its supreme claim for being, there are some perils involved in it. The larger freedom fostered here develops strength and power in those having capacities to utilize this freedom aright, but it is often disastrous to those who are deficient in the natural endowments for which such a life is intended. Every educator has learned from sad experience that college life is not intended for everyone. Undoubtedly, there are those that are actually harmed by such an environment. Young people often come to college who have not made adequate preparation in high school. These always become administrative problems. But the number that does not possess, previous to enrolment in a college or university, the background of inheritance, formulated habits, and experience required to profit by these opportunities is far greater than the number that is deficient in subject-matter knowledge.

Just as the time comes in the life of the young bird in the nest when it must test the strength of its wings for flight, so is every student confronted with the necessity of testing every mental, physical, and moral quality for rational living. The other day, I found in the garden of my home a young bird that had made its way out of its nest and attempted to fly. But its wing feathers were not adequate to the task and it had fallen a helpless mass to the ground. That experience is duplicated thousands of times in nature. Strength and

[109]

weakness, capacity and incapacity, courage and fear, confidence and a lack of confidence are physical and mental qualities that every living thing must cope with in the complicated process of living. Survival or destruction is often determined by them. The triumphs and the tragedies of life are predetermined by these characteristics. By the very conditions of college life, they are in daily evidence on every campus.

Even those who come to college with the strength of character and the knowledge to do acceptable work are often handicapped because of wrong notions of what is expected of them. I sometimes think that there is a conspiracy—unconscious, of course—between various elements in civic communities to keep students from getting off to a good start in college. Young people like you are in great danger of getting the urge to attend college because of secondary rather than primary considerations. The things you hear most about in the months preceding your entrance into college are usually secondary and relatively unimportant.

A conversation between a small group of mothers concerning their sons, who were away in college, was recently reproduced in one of our papers. One of them said to the others:

"My son graduates from college this spring but he has had a discouraging time in school. He went out for football during his freshman year but was not physically strong enough to make the team. The next year he did his best to get on the baseball team but for some reason the coach did not use him. In his junior year he applied for dance manager but the committee, after trying him out, said that he was awkward and could never make a good dancer. There was nothing left for him in his senior year but the valedictory. He took that, but he feels the disgrace keenly."

There are actually some parents like that, but I imagine

that most of your parents will not think you a failure if you make Phi Eta Sigma in your freshman year or Phi Beta Kappa in your senior year. I would not,have you think that I regard physical exercise as unimportant. The actual fact is that the great majority of students give too little thought to keeping their bodies in good physical condition while in college. I would urge you to take systematic exercise daily; but, as someone has said, jumping at conclusions and running up bills cannot be classified as exercise. These are not the things to which I refer.

It is not surprising that students often get the wrong perspective of college life. It not infrequently happens that even before students actually enter college their thoughts are directed to irrelevant things, which mislead them and often cause a misdirection of effort.

A few days ago, I read an advertisement in the *Chicago Tribune*, which illustrates the thought I have in mind. A large firm was making an appeal to prospective college girls to buy their college wardrobes at this store. As an incentive to visit the store, the management announced that several college graduates would be available to answer a number of "important" questions whose answers every girl should know. Some of the questions were as follows:

"How can I make the most effective picture when I stand on the observation platform and wave good-by to the boy I leave behind me?

"How can I be sure my favorite sorority will rush me like mad?

"What will make me look demure but devastating in my economics class?

"When the football captain looks my way how can I snag him from under the nose of fair hero worshippers?

"What can I do to convince my professor of my superior intelligence?

"At a prom, how shall I go about acquiring a fraternity pin?

"How, oh how, shall I have the grandest year I've ever had on the most limited allowance?"

This advertisement was, no doubt, prepared by a specialist who is presumed to know the psychology of advertising. The author assumed that he was asking the questions in which the college girl would be most interested, and I am not entirely sure that he was not correct. I am afraid if I had been preparing these questions as a means of attracting prospective college girls to a particular store, I would not have rated high as an advertising specialist.

Some of you may be surprised to know that colleges and universities were not established for the purpose of enabling you to affiliate with a social fraternity. Some of you are probably under the impression that a college is intended primarily to provide a place where fraternal connections may be established. Let me remind you that a social fraternity is a congenial place for a group of students to live while attending college. While they have come to occupy an important place in the life of our larger colleges and universities, they are quite incidental to the primary purpose for which educational institutions were established. You are not to infer from this statement that I am antagonistic to Greek-letter societies; but the fact that many students while in college, and even some college graduates, overemphasize their fraternal affiliations causes me to direct your attention to the proper place for social fraternities in college life. To the extent that social fraternities foster scholarship and promote high standards of conduct, they are important aids to educational endeavor; to the extent that they discourage scholarship and develop extravagant tastes, they are harmful. I urge you, therefore, to think of your fraternity connection in its proper relationship to the larger interests of the institution and to the student body as a whole.

Let it be understood, therefore, that your presence here is not primarily to make a Greek-letter fraternity, become a social leader, gain prominence as an athlete, acquire a fraternity pin, or convince your professors of your superior intelligence. Some of these things are well enough in their way, but all of them are incidental to the supreme purpose of acquiring knowledge and through the acquisition of knowledge discovering what is best in your mentality.

If learning, then, is the primary purpose of your being here, you should clearly conceive of its dual function. Every legitimate task before you should lead to new discoveries— discoveries of knowledge and discoveries of self. Learning has been defined as "the process whereby experiences are gained which function effectively in meeting new situations." It is quite obvious that a university community is not the only place where learning can be acquired, but it is the place where the entire set-up is designed to give the range of experiences which will help one to "function effectively" when confronted with new and untried situations. Education, sometimes, is defined as the process of adapting oneself to his environment. An educational institution where the learning process is fostered is designed to provide exactly the character of experiences that one needs to give mastery over changing environmental conditions.

Every university worthy of the name attempts to set up standards by which we measure conduct and intellectual accomplishment. The ultimate ends were first formulated by the Greeks in terms of beauty, goodness, and truth. Beauty is the synthesis of art. Goodness is the synthesis of religion. Truth is the synthesis of science. A knowledge of form, proportion, and symmetry is essential to an appreciation of art. A knowledge of man's relation to God and his fellow-men is essential to religion. A knowledge of design in nature and the laws governing animate and inanimate

[113]

matter is essential to an understanding of science. In final analysis, the supreme equation with which you are to work in all the courses and all the departments in this university may be formulated as follows:

Art + Science + Religion = Beauty + Truth + Goodness.

As far as human resources have made it possible, the university has been designed to typify this formula. This campus is one of the beauty spots of Oklahoma. Every tree, shrub and flower has been planted with loving care in a way to promote a sense of the beautiful and to harmonize with every other object about it. The buildings and equipment, so far as resources will permit, have been designed to create a love for truth and appreciation for goodness. You are invited to utilize these resources for what the ancients designated as the *summum bonum*, which they never ceased to search for at the height of their glory and which we are to search for as we struggle upward toward the levels of the highest accomplishment.

Let us think of our progress toward an appreciation of art, the exemplification of goodness, and the conquest of truth in terms of achievement. One of the greatest social philosophers that America has produced and a former professor of mine, the late Dr. Albion W. Small of the University of Chicago, classified these achievements as follows:

1. Achievement in promoting health
2. Achievement in producing wealth
3. Achievement in harmonizing human relations
4. Achievement in discovery and spread of knowledge
5. Achievement in the fine arts
6. Achievement in religion

Education, in the large, is concerned with achievement—achievement in all of these realms of human endeavor. Life is lived at the highest level by those who have achieved

[114]

high rating in all of these. But few of us ever have our lives enriched by the conquests of all these aspects of achievement. It not infrequently happens that the wealthy man is frail physically. The scholar—the man of learning—is often a social recluse, the artist is frequently too subjective to be human, and the devout man of God is often prejudiced against knowledge. Learning, therefore, as a function of education, is the process by which every life is pre-empted of all its capacities in the attainment of beauty, goodness, and truth.

When I think of education in these terms, I find it difficult to be tolerant with the student who is indifferent to his educational opportunities and who is willing to trifle away his time in the midst of such an environment. I am equally intolerant of the college professor who uses the precious hours assigned to classroom instruction in profitless discussion of irrelevant subjects. Lord Chesterfield was right when he said in one of his letters to his son while a student at Leipzig that "every moment you now lose is so much character and advantage lost; on the other hand, every moment you now employ usefully, is so much time wisely laid out, at prodigious interest." The period is relatively short for acquiring a college education and the time should be utilized in the most profitable ways.

My remarks have been predicated on the theory that all of you are young intellectuals who are now interested in being discovered—discovered for a purpose. Learning is not an end in itself. The acquisition of knowledge is not even the end of learning. There is a more important objective. All the knowledge that may be acquired through the learning process should be utilized for the purpose of self-evaluation.

The university is a great focus for testing life from all angles. Just as the Olympic games at Los Angeles this summer tested the relative skill and endurance of the greatest athletes of the world, likewise every educational institution is an intellectual marathon where students are daily testing out their relative intellectual, moral, physical, and spiritual qualities. It is in this environment that you have the opportunity of measuring yourselves in relation to the outer world of material objects or the inner world of thought and emotion. Learning in this sense should become exhilarating and an alluring adventure into self-consciousness. You will find that it has its hazards as well as its conquests; but for those with courage, initiative, and perseverance, the hazards are negligible and the rewards are indescribably great.

The supreme need of the times is men and women with will power to do right and resist wrong, to think clearly and to act wisely, and to respect the rights of others as they expect others to respect their rights. There is no better place in the world to acquire these supreme qualities than in an environment of this kind. An "intelligent ordering of experience," to use a phrase of James Truslow Adams, is both a duty and an opportunity. "You do not educate a man by telling him what he knew not," says John Ruskin, "but by making him what he was not." This is another way of saying that every man should so direct his experiences that right conduct will be the natural result of right thinking. The university will not do enough for you or you will not get enough out of your experiences here unless this ideal is realized.

Finally, let me remind you that this will be a critical year in the history of the university. The existence of the institution depends entirely upon the good will of the citizenship of this state. As you know, people everywhere have been suffering great financial hardships and they have been experiencing great anxieties. A psychological state of mind like this tends to cause men to lose a sense of relative values. At this moment the determination of the American people to reduce the cost of government is likely to result in the automatic reduction of expenditures, irrespective of how it may affect public welfare or the future of our civilization. You can do much this year to prevent disaster coming to the university. There are some of our people who honestly believe that many students who come to our institutions of higher learning do not profit by the advantages that have been provided for them. You alone can discredit this popular belief by making the most of your opportunities this year. Idleness and indifference are always to be discouraged, not only in college, but out of it. The time, however, has come when indifference to the serious purposes of education cannot be tolerated. You are to see to it that nothing occurs during this year that will bring reproach upon the good name of the student body or the institution that nurtures you.

Let us, therefore, as we learn, receive, and hear give preference in our lives to the things that are true, the things that are honest, the things that are just, and the things that are pure, to the end that happiness to you and satisfaction and pride to those who sent you here may result from this year's work.

LEARNING *AND* LEISURE[1]

CHAPTER TEN

A LITTLE more than three months ago I presented diplomas in this hall to nearly a thousand students. Many of those who graduated at that time entered college in September, 1929—about the time of the great stock market crash. As I faced that great group of graduating seniors on that June morning, I found myself thinking of the changes that have come over the world in the four years that these students had been in college. An era of unprecedented prosperity had closed with registration days in 1929. The four years that followed were characterized by indescribable distress. The carefree years of the nineteen-twenties had been followed by years of anxiety and suffering. Those who were graduating on that eventful day in their lives were to go into a vastly different world from whence they came when they entered college.

Many of you who are entering college for the first time today, no doubt, are looking forward to your graduation in 1937. You are probably selecting your courses with a view to your needs when college days are over. What kind of a social order will confront you as you go forth from college? What opportunities will you have in the vocation or profession for which you are now beginning to make preparation? There is implied in the selection of your courses of study a

1. Convocational address delivered at the opening of the forty-second academic year on September 19, 1933.

[118]

prophecy of the future. Upon the accuracy of your insight will depend your future happiness, as well as your success. Events are reshaping human affairs with such rapidity that it is difficult to predict world conditions a few years hence. It is reasonable to assume, in the light of what is happening today, that the world into which you will go after your graduation will be vastly different from what it is today. This dynamic situation makes it exceedingly difficult to select a course of study in preparation for the needs and requirements of the years that are ahead.

Thoughts and habits are changing so rapidly today that it is impossible to appraise their consequences. The fact that these changes are being accelerated by ballyhoo and noisy demonstration does not lessen their significance. We see things happening today that we have never seen before. An irresponsible individualism is being superseded rapidly by regulated and co-operative capitalism. It is profoundly significant that an individualistic society can surrender a long and cherished conception of life and can accept almost overnight a radically different philosophy, involving mass action and group consciousness.

The growing conflict between individualism and collectivism was discussed by Dr. Charles W. Eliot in his Barbour-Page Foundation lectures at the University of Virginia in 1909. According to this great intellectual American, "individualism values highly not only the rights of the single person, but also the initiative of the individual left free by society. Collectivism values highly social rights, objects to an individual initiative which does mischief when left free, holds that the interest of the many should override the interest of the individual, whenever the two interests conflict, and should control social action, and yet does not propose to extinguish the individual, but only to restrict him for the common good, including his own." After pointing out the strong natural hold that individualism had on American democracy, Dr. Eliot contended that individualism was slowly losing ground in its conflict with collectivism and prophesied that ultimately it would be overcome by its protagonist. That prophecy has been fulfilled in our day.

The conflict between individualism and collectivism in education has been going on for a long time. In the past, education was directed to the needs of the individual child. Montaigne developed his theory of education around the interest of a single gifted child whose intellectual life was guided by one capable tutor. He never thought in terms of mass education. While Rousseau approached the problem somewhat differently, he had very much the same idea. Thomas Jefferson founded the University of Virginia upon the ideal of free choice of subjects and the personal wishes of the student. Ezra Cornell, the founder of the great university that bears his name, expressed the wish that the institution should be a place where anyone might pursue any subject that appealed to him.

The spirit of collectivism has made many inroads in recent times upon this individualistic conception. The fact that the collective interest of society often promotes individual welfare has made it easy to move in this direction. Compulsory education, restriction on the choice of subjects, and state adoption of textbooks are examples of the tendency toward collective action in education. The collective interest of society was responsible for the establishment of state-supported institutions of higher learning; and their courses of study, while apparently designed to meet individual needs, have been primarily determined by social objectives. In recent times, we have seen all kinds of arbitrary standards set up for admission to state-supported institutions and very definite legal requirements for the practice of the professions. The latest steps in collective action are restrictions on enrolment and limitation of numbers in various professional courses. There is much to indicate that this tendency will be carried further in the immediate future. It is fortunate, of course, that many of the restrictions upon individualism have been brought about through the co-operation between collective and individualistic influences. Bertrand Russell, in his recent book *Education and the Modern World*, says: "A sense of citizenship, of social co-operation, is therefore more necessary than it used to be; but it remains important that this should be secured without too great a diminution of individual judgment and individual initiative." It is certainly questionable how much further collectivism in education can go without infringing seriously upon the rights, as well as the needs of the individual. There is a need for the searching of hearts in the future consideration of all these tendencies in American life.

Collectivism in business, as reflected in the several industrial codes recently promulgated by the National Recovery Administration and accepted by industrial enterprises, raises the question of restriction on individualism in education. Will state-supported educational institutions, for example, be utilized to promulgate popular theories of political practices? We have seen this brought about in a most ruthless manner in Germany recently. Acceptance of a particular conception of governmental policy has been made the basis of employment rather than intellectual attainments, character and personality. A similar attitude has prevailed in Italy for some years. Of course, we do not expect to see this happen in America, but these examples illustrate the extreme to which collective action may go under the domination of a Hitler or a Mussolini.

Whatever view we may hold with reference to the limitations of collectivism on education, there can be no question that our educational institutions have an obligation to the social order. Our schools are functional agencies of society. As such, they must adjust their objectives and conform their programs to the changing world that they are designed to serve. There is a popular belief that our educational institutions have not always fulfilled their obligations to society, but anyone who is familiar with the changing objectives of education in America during the last hundred years must be convinced that our schools have made a serious effort to adjust their curricula to the changing social situation.

The changes that are taking place today impose new obligations, as well as new opportunities, upon our schools. The national recovery program is bringing about important changes in the lives of our people. The industrial codes that are being formulated in conformity with this program are limiting the hours of labor to 35 or 40, out of a total of 168 hours for the week. This releases the energies of thousands of people to be utilized in other than breadwinning employment. Is this free time to become a social asset or a social liability? The misuse of unhired time is as serious a problem as the unwise use of wealth. Sociologists and others have recognized this fact for years, but it has taken an unprecedented crime wave and a state of demoralization never experienced before in our history to drive the fact home to all of us.

Throughout our history, we have glorified work. The willingness to work and the ability to do good work have been recognized as supreme virtues. John Ruskin expressed the thought in one connection as follows: "Every man should do good work for his bread and every man should have good bread for his work." The pioneer spirit in America gave validity to this accepted code. In our early history, men had to work hard to live and the lazy idler was regarded as a social drone. It was a necessity during pioneer days that a man who did not work should not eat. In those days survival and security depended upon everyone working hard, spending sparingly, and saving rigorously. The virtues of work, thrift, and sobriety have endured as supreme social values.

These verities have not been discarded, but their position in the hierarchy of virtues has changed. Machinery and industrial organization have been for a generation constantly increasing the efficiency of man power. The results have produced consequences of great significance. It is claimed that automatic machines and organization methods make it possible today to dispense with one third of all the 48,832,589 workers listed as gainfully employed in 1930, and to produce sufficient goods to maintain the present standard of living and only require the average employee to work thirty-six hours a week.

This situation has not only produced a reappraisal of the social virtues, but it has changed our estimates of social values. In the past, we have measured success by the possession of worldly goods. Prestige and power have always gone to those who possessed large wealth. Idleness and wasteful display have been the evidence of economic surplus. It is now a possibility that a new conception of social values may appear. Is it too much to expect in the future that prestige may come to those who use their leisure for the enrichment of personal and social life? The time may be at hand when the making of a great life may be recognized as at least as important as the making of a great fortune. There is wisdom in the words of an eminent sociologist who has said recently: "We must face and welcome a world in which leisure is more important than money making and where both earning and spending will be judged by the quality of life they produce, rather than by the wealth, the power, the excitement or the display."

The proper use of leisure time is not a new problem to us. Shorter working hours have come to thousands in recent years. When industry, business and transportation accepted the eight-hour day, the proper use of leisure time became a popular topic for discussion. Dr. L. P. Jacks predicted in a lecture at Glasgow University that the hours needed for mass production and mechanized labor would fall so low as "to leave the leisure hours the major quantity" for all classes of workers. This prophecy has probably been fulfilled much earlier than he realized at the time. Dr. Jacks has said more recently: "I name education for leisure as an outstanding need of the present age." Quite recently Mr. H. G. Wells, in his monumental book entitled *The Work, Wealth and Happiness of Mankind,* surveys the history of the increase and possibilities of leisure time. "One inevitable consequence of continuing human progress," he says, "is a steady increase of human leisure and human resources." Mr. C. E. M. Joad has written a little book entitled *Diogenes or the Future of Leisure,* in which he surveys the place of leisure time in modern civilization. But the industrial codes that have been promulgated in recent weeks by the Federal Government bring the problem of leisure time squarely before us as one requiring serious consideration. The *New York Times,* in a recent editorial, has said that "a code looking to the better education of the people in a sensible use of their leisure time may, as one has suggested, come in time to be known as a second Magna Charta of liberty." That education for leisure is as necessary as training for work is recognized by all those who have given serious consideration to the problem.

In fact, there is an intimate interrelation between work and leisure. The use made of free time has an important influence upon the quality of employed time. The reverse is not equally true, but the proper attitude toward one's vocation should give direction to one's avocational and

[124]

recreational activities. Dr. Jacks believes that if an individual makes all the proper adjustments in life, he should make work and play essentially interchangeable. The wise employer will, therefore, be concerned about what his employees do during their unhired time. No argument is necessary to sustain the contention that a man who spends his free time in exhausting frivolity cannot render a high quality of service during his working hours.

It is equally true that a student's use of his free time largely determines his accomplishments in college. It is not an exaggeration to say that a student's grades are, in general, the result of the use he makes of his week-ends and holidays rather than by his regularity in attending classes. Learning is a serious business. The acquisition and the assimilation of knowledge involve much more than reading textbooks and listening to a professor's exposition of his subject. No man or woman can acquire an education by attending classes fifteen or sixteen hours a week. Learning involves much more than this. It involves a state of mind, as well as conformity to a schedule of instruction. Dissipation of any kind is the antidote to learning. The Greek word for school (σχολή) means leisure, the Latin word for college (*collegium*) means bringing together or assembling, while study (*studium*) means effort. A school, then, is a place of leisurely meditation where a group of earnest young people are assembled for sustained effort in the acquisition of knowledge. Perhaps this definition sounds far-fetched to you. A more accurate definition, according to the general impression of many people, might be stated as follows: A school is a place where a group of young people is assembled and required to attend lectures, in which few of them are interested, for five days, during which they plan for their week-end parties or automobile trips to neighboring cities. But this is not the classical conception of what an educational institution should be. The poet Wordsworth, in one of his sonnets, described quite accurately what the trouble is with our educational institutions. He says:

"The world is too much with us; late and soon,
  Getting and spending, we lay waste our powers."

The world *is* too much with us these days. It is difficult to keep from dissipating our powers of mind and heart in profitless and wasteful activities. My point is that both in industry and education the use we make of our free time determines to a large extent our success in scheduled hours of work.

The development of the whole man—body, mind, heart and soul—has long been accepted as a comprehensive task of education. We now need to realize that education must take into account the entire time at the disposal of man in the fulfillment of this task. Our educational system, up to the present, has done little more than prepare man to utilize approximately a third of his time. Many of the evils in our society are due to the fact that we have ignored the other two thirds of the twenty-four hours at our disposal. The late Arnold Bennett wrote a remarkable book some years ago entitled *How to Live on Twenty-four Hours a Day*. He tells us we have only this much time extended over an uncertain number of days, months and years in which "to spin health, pleasure, money, content, respect and the evolution of an immortal soul." The thought running through this book is that man needs to live well for every second, minute and hour of each full day, and not merely for a fractional part of this time.

Professor Walter B. Pitkin, of Columbia University, tells us in his recent book entitled *Life Begins at Forty* that "everybody comes into the world with a certain chance of acquiring a working capital of a round half million. Half million what? Half million hours, of course. They will be on hand, ready for investment, as fast as the new-born promoter crawls from his cradle and toddles forth to meet the dawn. They will be paid in full if he is skillful enough and lucky enough to stick around until he turns the mossy corner of three score years and ten.

"He can not give away his minutes. He can not borrow minutes from a friend. He can not steal minutes. Money is a mere medium of exchange. Time is neither a medium nor is it exchangeable. It is the inmost stuff of life itself."

This may sound quite quixotic, but there is wisdom in these thoughts. Our inalienable and universal heritage is time—a sufficient amount of it to produce a great life. We cannot dispose of it. We must consume it. But the methods of consumption determine whether we are to be ignorant or scholarly, wise or foolish, successes or failures, libertines or gentlemen.

Youth needs guidance in the use of this priceless inheritance. Avocational and recreational education comes into the picture to supply this need. The industrial revolution produced the vocational objective in education more than a half century ago. The economic revolution of today brings us squarely to the need for avocational and recreational education. Educational institutions will not abandon the older aims, but new conditions will subordinate them in point of emphasis. We have already found that training for a single vocation is unwise. Demand for skilled workers is shifting rapidly. The times call for versatile workers. This means many adjustments in educational policy.

We need to recall the magnificent contributions that men have made in leisure pursuits to science, art, literature and public welfare. Leonardo da Vinci was an artist, but his varied structural designs have caused him to be called the father of engineering and aëronautics. Chaucer was a collector of customs, but his poetry has made him immortal.

[127]

Benjamin Franklin was a printer; but his title to fame rests on his literary accomplishments, his scientific discoveries and his statesmanship. Mendel was an abbot of a monastery, but his place in the sun is due to his contributions to genetics. Van Leeuwenhoek, the great Dutch scientist and the author of *Arcana Naturae*, was a merchant. Fabre was a teacher of the classics in France, but observations made by him in his back yard gave him world-wide recognition as an entomologist. Priestley, the discoverer of oxygen, was a preacher with an impediment in his speech. His interest in scientific research probably caused him to inflict many a poor sermon upon his parishioners; but if it had not been for his avocational interest, Priestley would never have been heard of beyond the confines of his local parish. These are only a few of the names of men who have enriched the world in one field or another by having some abiding interest outside the work they performed for their daily bread. Much of the world's best work through all the ages has been done by men outside the hours of their regular employment.

The idle time now being consumed by irresponsible people who are depressed, desperate or delinquent must be conserved for constructive leisure. If this free time, which is the priceless possession of thousands today, could be utilized properly, the sum total of human happiness would be greatly enlarged. The problem, of course, is a partnership one, in which both society and the individual must share. Countless thousands of people today, who are unemployed, desire to work and to earn not only subsistence for themselves, but a surplus that might be used in profitable ways. This is society's responsibility, and the fact that after all these centuries man has not been able through organized effort to prevent these cycles of widespread unemployment is a severe indictment of his insight and ingenuity. On the other hand, the individual, as a partner in the social group, has not always been wise in the use of his full time when conditions enabled him to acquire a surplus of this world's goods. Insurance against periodic unemployment, shorter working hours, and a wage scale sufficiently high to create a surplus are society's responsibilities to the individual at this time. With this security the home, the school and the church should face seriously the task of training men and women to utilize every hour of the twenty-four at their disposal in the interest of public welfare and individual happiness.

This means that avocational and recreational education must be assigned a place in the curriculum equal in dignity with courses in vocational and professional education in every college and university in the land. This, of course, means a rather thorough reorganization of existing programs of study. But the time has come when courses must be adapted to the needs of students rather than made to conform to the interest and predilections of faculty groups.

Both character and knowledge are required to render acceptable service in positions of public trust. Deficiency in these qualities accounts for scandals and inefficiency that are constantly occurring in public life. The mismanagement of our city governments, the shortsightedness of school board officials, and numerous other services of this character are due to these causes. If our public school system is to hold its place in popular esteem and justify the theory on which it is sustained, it is absolutely necessary for it to train men and women to serve the public with competency, devotion and honesty. I admit this is not a very original thought, but it never needed emphasis more than it does today.

I am making a distinction between avocational and recreational education. The two concepts are usually thought of as different aspects of one thing, but to my way of thinking they are quite different. Avocational education, to me, means training for useful public service that is no part of regular employment and for which the individual receives little, if any, remuneration. Recreational education is training one to enjoy his free time largely for his own benefit. Avocational education has a social objective, while recreational education is concerned with the individual's needs and requirements.

Recently a prominent American citizen said in a mild criticism of the NRA that every man had an inalienable right to work eight hours a day. I recall that in the late years of the nineteenth century men were saying that a man's time was his own and that he had a right to work as many hours a day as he desired. There is both truth and error in these generalizations. I freely admit that if a man cannot or will not profitably utilize his free time for wholesome ends, it is better for him to be employed than to be idle. This conclusion, though logical, need not follow. Men can be taught and directed to utilize their unemployed time in just as profitable ways as they can be taught to utilize their employed time efficiently and well. The tragedy in American life is that so few mature men can get satisfaction out of leisure hours. Professor Pitkin, in the book previously quoted, brings out this fact. There are many forms of recreation that give satisfaction to those who participate in them. Travel, reading, conversation (now nearly a lost art), walking, swimming, golfing and numerous other activities are profitable ways of utilizing leisure time. A man does not have to be a professional athlete to enjoy a wholesome game. I have been playing golf for many years. I do not recall having ever won a foursome, but I have found great enjoyment in the game and some of the friendships I value most in life have been made on the golf course.

It has long been my belief that every college student should be taught at least two games that he could play with enjoyment after his graduation. But this type of education is not more important than education for travel, reading, music, and art appreciation, and many others too numerous to mention that contribute to enjoyment and contentment. It is fortunate, indeed, that at a time when the energies of thousands are being released from arduous toil there should be so many profitable and interesting ways to utilize leisure time. The radio, picture shows, museums, art galleries, dramatic productions, playgrounds, national parks, inexpensive means of travel and a thousand other agencies for profitable enjoyment are available to all.

A new synthesis of values needs to be made—something similar to what Plato called harmony and Aristotle happiness. The *summum bonum* is to be found in a new appraisal of work, play, love and worship. This new appraisal is your chief task as you begin this new college year. The earnestness and fidelity with which you pursue the work at hand and the ways by which you utilize your leisure time will indicate to what extent you are really preparing to live the good and useful life in the world into which you will go in a few fleeting years.

Much more is involved than the making of high grades or avoiding contact with the faculty committee on conduct. You are expected to live a life characterized by high purpose. The thing that gives supreme value to college life is that it is the one place in society where all the powers of mind and heart have an opportunity for exercise and development. The fact that you have a wide range of choices of conduct does not mean that you are to choose the easy or the sordid way.

You are expected to learn to live here as well as to learn to know. Learning to live well is as important as to learn the subject matter of books. But one is not contradictory of the other. They are supplementary rather than contradictory. The life of thought should re-enforce the life of action. Time is at your disposal. It is your priceless heritage, and this college environment is your supreme opportunity to consume it day after day in the making of a good and useful life.

THE DUALISM IN LEARNING[1]

CHAPTER ELEVEN

NINE YEARS ago I delivered my first convocational address at the opening of the college year. On that occasion I attempted to emphasize the primary purpose of a college education. In the opening days of each successive year since that time, I have discussed some aspect of learning. The changing student body and the time interval between these discussions have made the continuity of thought impossible. But I have tried to keep in mind the fact that the acquisition of knowledge is the supreme task confronting students as they enter upon a college career, and the primary cause that should bring them to college. This happens to be the concluding discussion of the topic that I began in 1925, and I am inviting you today to think with me about one of the most important aspects of the learning process.

Every educational program worthy of acceptation recognizes and comprehends the dualism in education. Preparation for a vocational or professional career should be inextricably associated with preparation for rational living. It is a lamentable fact that not all those who teach or enrol in college recognize this duality in learning.

There are two schools of thought with reference to the objectives of higher education. One school believes that

1. Convocational address delivered at the opening of the forty-third academic year on September 18, 1934.

[133]

higher education should not concern itself with anything except the search for and acquisition of knowledge. The other school believes that education should be concerned with the discovery of knowledge and the harmonious development of the physical, intellectual, moral, and spiritual attributes of the individual. A distinguished university president, writing in an important magazine, said some time ago: "Universities have developed the idea in parents, or parents have developed it in universities, that the institution is in some way responsible for the moral, social, physical, and intellectual welfare of the student. This is very nice for the parents; it is hard on the universities for besides being expensive, it deflects them from their main task, which is the advancement of knowledge." This statement is followed by the suggestion that "the university must take the position that the student should not be sent to the university unless he is independent and intelligent enough to go there." A leading literary publication, in commenting on this quotation, says: "In America, the proponents of 'character development' have produced the 'beef-eater,' whose 'muscular Christianity' became a byword to the 'esthete.' . . . . 'Character' has produced hundreds of graduates—names on request, though the interrogator must be sworn to secrecy—with the brainpans of dinosaurs, graduates who lumber about in the grooves set for them in adolescence. Fruitful thinkers along social lines developed by the American universities have, by and large, been the few fortunate souls who have escaped the character-moulding processes." These quotations fairly represent the point of view of those who think that character building should be no concern of the university.

The other school of thought takes exactly the opposite view. Those who belong to this school of thought believe that every life, in order to be lived worthily, needs conscious direction. It is assumed, of course, that emphasis on moral training should vary during the student's progress from home life to high school, from high school to college, and from college to the university. There is no question that the place of largest emphasis should fall within the home circle; but character development is indissolubly connected with the enlarging experiences of youth and, therefore, cannot be terminated at some arbitrary stage in a youth's physical development or intellectual progress.

It should be clearly understood that the word "character," as it is used today, is of rather recent connotation. The word meant quite a different thing to the Greek philosophers and to the Roman writers, who succeeded them. But intellectuals through the ages have magnified the attributes that enter into our definition of character today. The fact is, there is no way to dissociate moral training from intellectual accomplishment. There is no genuine pursuit of knowledge that does not involve the qualities of honesty of effort, love of truth, fidelity to high purpose, and a passion for the public good. To attempt even to dissociate research from these qualities would be to sterilize knowledge and to make its benefits ineffective. In other words, there is an intimate dualism in the learning process; and to disregard either one or the other in the educational process is nothing short of heresy.

It has been relatively easy in modern times to emphasize vocational education at the expense of culture. Success has been measured very largely in terms of worldly goods. Students have felt the need of preparing for a technical calling or a profession as a means of getting on in the world. Our institutions of higher learning have made every possible preparation to provide adequate facilities for training in these fields. The enormous productivity of the American people is largely due to the service rendered by our educational institutions in preparing men and women to meet the diversified demands of a materialistic age. No one would disparage this accomplishment or decrease the facilities that are now available for performing this task; but in the highly industrialized society, of which we are all a part, it has been quite easy for us to forget that learning to live is just as important as learning to make a living. To fail in either is to invite disaster, both to the individual and to society. I would, therefore, this morning place emphasis on this dualism in learning as a means of emphasizing what I have said in previous addresses on this subject.

The whole educational process is designed to adapt the individual to live in perfect adjustment to his environment. No man can live a satisfactory life unless he can conform his behavior to the social situation in which he finds himself. We designate those as antisocial who rebel against the established social order. We designate those as leaders who are constantly engaged in the struggle of modifying the social structure as a means of better adapting it to the needs and requirements of organized society. Between the antisocial individual and the group leader live the countless thousands who docilely conform to the social order as it is or who live complacently on the margin between conformity and non-conformity. Education at all levels is designed to develop all the moral stamina and intellectual powers possessed by the individual to the end that he may live peaceably and contentedly with his neighbors.

When we think of the complexity of organized society it is not surprising that it takes long years of preparation to accomplish the task. The long period of infancy is explained by this fact. Why is the human child so helpless at birth? Why is the period of adolescence so long? The biologist has answered these questions for us. Preparation for living in a complex world requires both time and adequate training. John Fisk in discussing the meaning of infancy says: "The difference between man and all other living

[136]

creatures in respect to teachableness, progressiveness, and individuality of character" is due to the relatively long plastic period of physical and mental growth. Newell Dwight Hillis once expressed this doctrine eloquently in these words: "In proportion as man goes toward God, he lengthens his childhood. A sand fly is mature in three days, a robin in three months, a colt in three years, but man requires three climacterics of seven years each. This long epoch of childhood and growth involved in twenty-one years makes it possible for society to hand over to the growing soul all the treasures accumulated in three thousand years." The dual demand for learning to live and learning to make a living is not to be accomplished in a day or a year. This is the lesson that we learn from biological development and physiological and mental changes.

The fact that so many people live on such a low plane is an indication that it requires thought and discrimination, as well as time, to make life worth while. Rudolf Eucken, who was professor of philosophy in the University of Jena for so many years, repeatedly directed attention to this thought in his lectures. In his book on *The Meaning and Value of Life*, he says that in order to live the good life, it is necessary to struggle against the baser motives that threaten our well-being. Life has both meaning and value, but the meaning of life is to be discovered and the value of life is to be acquired through effort. Martin Luther said in one connection: "There is no finished achievement; all is in the making. We do not see the end, but only the road. The full splendor is not yet, but the refining work goes on." The challenge that comes to each of us is in the recognition of this unfinished achievement. Life is always in the making. Knowledge and experience should be constantly utilized in refining conduct and in giving direction to our endeavors. This is what education is for. If we miss this compelling motive in our progress toward educational accomplishment,

[137]

we are sure to lose our way and miss the supreme satisfaction that a college environment offers. In the language of Euripides, "who so neglects learning in his youth, loses the past and is dead for the future."

It is hard for the average youth to realize that life is no idle game. Too many students are inclined to live irresponsible lives. It is so easy to follow the line of least resistance in an environment where so much is being done for you. But I would remind you again that learning to live requires toil, renunciation, and sacrifice. This axiomatic truth seems, I am sure, rather questionable to the youth of today. Has not the inventive skill of man been utilized to reduce the burdens of toil? Is not the gratification of the appetite regarded more of a virtue today than abstinence? Why sacrifice for others when every one is getting all he can for himself? These questions naturally arise in times like these. But there are no biographies being written about the lives of men who followed the easy path or who took the road of least resistance. The great and near great paid the full price in their youth for great achievement.

It often happens that students think of college days merely as a time of preparation for living in the future. They forget that life must be lived every day and that responsibility increases as the range of one's choices enlarges. A student cannot live a cloistered life in a modern university of higher learning. The relationships in an environment such as this offer both perils and opportunities. Every hour of every day in college gives opportunities to make choices, many of them new to past experience. Even in these opening days courses of study are being selected, new friendships are being formed, opportunity to participate in some amusement or sport is offered—all of these are important and the choices that are made in all these ranges of experience will have an important bearing upon the formation of character and the course of future conduct. The

[138]

discrimination that is used in all these matters will test life in significant ways and determine very largely future courses of action.

In some respects, college life takes on the characteristics of a political or economic crisis. It is a time of disillusionment and self-revelation. When life is lived adventurously or anxiously, there is always a searching of hearts and an appraisal of human values. I think, for example, we are a wiser people as a result of the lean years through which we have been passing. We have certainly been disillusioned about our economic security.

In the years of prosperity following the World War, it was customary to boast about our country being the richest nation in the world. Pride of possession made us vain and self-possessed. America is still a land of great wealth, both actual and potential; but "the years of the locust" have purged us of false pride and self-complacency. This period of hardship and distress has done something for us that is even more significant. It has made us conscious of our inner thoughts and motives. I recall seeing in the Hall of Science at the Centennial Exposition at Chicago a human figure made of glass in which every muscle, blood vessel, and organ of the body were perfectly transparent through a system of delicately adjusted electric lights. A crisis, such as war or economic depression, does a similar thing for the character of man. It causes us to take an inward look at ourselves, which is revealing and often surprising. It does even more than this. The conditions of life enable us better to appraise and understand the motives and the qualities of our friends and associates.

I have repeatedly been told by soldiers who participated in the World War that they were astonished sometimes to learn when the zero hour came that some of the men with whom they had been associating during the period of routine military training were not what they thought them to be. When the eventful hour arrived for them to go over the top to face the hail of bullets from the enemy, everything that was concealed of character and manhood was uncovered. It happened that some of the men who had not impressed them very favorably showed characteristics of courage and determination. It is the tragedy of every crisis that we find many men whom we have trusted and respected who are unworthy of confidence or esteem. These years of the depression have brought many disillusionments about the real character of many men in responsible places. We are familiar with the names of great banking executives who have defrauded their customers, of prominent professional men who have abused the confidence of their clients, of public officials who have used high office for private gain. This does not mean that a crisis increases the number of men of this character. It simply means that in critical times men are revealed as they are. The thing that should cheer our hearts and stimulate our optimism, however, is the fact that in the crises of the great war and the economic depression, there have been countless thousands of men who manifested remarkable courage and integrity.

College life is very much like this. The conditions under which students live make self-examination and self-revelation inevitable. Tests of character are constantly being made. Self-examinations are constantly going on. There are few students who spend four years in college who do not reveal themselves completely to their teachers and associates. There is, of course, tragedy as well as triumph produced by such an environment as this. But the discipline connected with the learning process has no higher function than that of persistent self-examination and self-revelation. Every individual, of course, knows in his heart whether he is honest or dishonest, truthful or untruthful, trustworthy or untrustworthy, courageous or cowardly, a libertine or a gentleman. Under normal conditions, it is possible to conceal these characteristics; but college life is not a normal environment. It is an environment especially designed to test the qualities of manhood and womanhood, to develop and strengthen character, and to fortify life at weak places.

The best discipline that can come to the morally weak is to know that one's imperfections of character are known to his associates. We are so constituted that we value the good opinions of others, especially those whom we admire. There is nothing so stimulating to the man of good character than the realization that his virtues are understood and appreciated by those with whom he associates. There is no character-forming influence quite so great as this sensitiveness to the esteem of our friends. The individual who is not sensitive to popular esteem is hopelessly deficient in pride.

But lest I be misunderstood, let me hasten to explain that men and women cannot be divided into arbitrary groups on the basis of character. Self-revelation is an incidental rather than a main objective of college life. Exposure to the learning process is primarily intended to discipline conduct, to correct false impressions, to conquer temptation, and to strengthen the texture of the human fabric. The student entering college should understand this and use every experience of his daily life to accomplish these results. It is too much to expect that students who come up to college will not make mistakes, that they will not make wrong choices at times, or that they will do everything exactly in the right way. If this were true, much that is being done in the name of education could be dispensed with. It would not be necessary to maintain a large personnel force to work with students. Even methods of instruction in some respects could be changed, but the fact that students are constantly testing out both strength and weakness where these qualities can be observed gives those responsible for their guidance an opportunity to serve them in profitable ways.

The whole educational process should aim at reducing the number of men and women whose lives are not characterized by consistency of purpose and unity of ideals. Bertrand Russell discusses this subject in his recent book on *Education and the Modern World*. He recognizes the dualism in education, however, for he says: "Education has, at all times, had a twofold aim, namely instruction, and training in good conduct." But in this book, he raises the question: Should education aim to produce the good citizen or the good individual? It is rather surprising that he takes the position that the education of the individual and the training of the citizen are entirely different things. It seems to me that they are not contradictory things, but merely different aspects of the same thing.

The good citizen is one who manifests a sense of social and civic responsibility, and the good individual is one who conforms his life to the best patterns of ethical standards. To imply that one is contradictory to the other seems to set up a false dualism in education. Lord Russell freely admits that good conduct varies with political institutions and social traditions of the community. There is certainly no way by which standards of conduct can be maintained in community life without reflecting these ideals into civic practices. False theories of education of this character have brought widespread criticism on the entire scheme of public education. The products of our schools and colleges have revealed too many inconsistencies between personal idealism and practical everyday conduct. Integrity in education implies a unity between theory and practice. Students must be taught that honesty, for example, cannot be departmentalized like goods in a ten-cent store. It is not one thing to cheat on an examination and quite another to be very conscientious about paying one's bills promptly. Men are not relatively honest, truthful, or sincere. They are either honest or dishonest, truthful or untruthful, sincere or insincere, and they cannot practice honesty in some relations of life and act dishonestly in others. They are not to tell the truth sometimes and falsify at other times. They are not to manifest a spirit of sincerity in the intimacies of family life and practice insincerity at dinner parties. Integrity is oneness of purpose predicated upon consistency in living.

If this doctrine is sound, much of our educational practice is indefensible. The whole theory of modern education is based on the policy of maintaining good standards of instruction in the classroom and forgetting all about the student after the class period is over. One sometimes hears college professors say that "it is my business to give good instruction to my students, and my responsibility ends when that is done." I am inclined to believe that is the general attitude of many men and women who teach in our colleges and universities. I not only think that this viewpoint is wrong, but I believe it is responsible for many of the evils that have grown up in our body politic. The statement is made in many of the catalogues of our institutions that two hours of preparation are required for every hour of formal instruction. This is one of the numerous fictions that educators perpetrate upon the innocent public. Every experienced educator knows that the average student does not devote two hours of preparation for each hour of lecture. We ought to do one of two things. We should either eliminate this incorrect statement from our catalogues or attempt to find a way to make the regulation effective. Parenthetically, I might say that I am not sure that two hours of preparation are necessary for every hour of class work. I think probably it should be necessary, but the wide range in the quality of instruction makes this policy indefensible. But we persistently limit the number of hours of classroom work or laboratory periods to fifteen or sixteen hours a week on the theory that thirty or thirty-two additional hours will be devoted to preparation, which, of course, would fully occupy all the time that the average student should devote to his college work a week. Most of the administrative difficulties with students result from the fact that standards of instruction do not make this necessary, and the large amount of free time left on the student's hands is responsible for many of the irregularities in student conduct.

One of two things should be done about this situation if the policy of requiring two hours of preparation for one of actual instruction is sound in principle. Either we should find a way to bring the standards of instruction up to such a uniform level that the student could not get on and pass his courses without devoting a sufficient amount of his free time to preparation, or colleges and universities should be so organized that definite direction could be given by the instructional staff for the guidance of students in their work outside of formal class instruction.

I am inclined to believe that the direction of the student's work during the informal hours of preparation is more important than the hours devoted to lectures. It is certain that what the student does for himself intellectually is more important than what someone does for him. I am not making a plea for regimentation in education. It is certainly unwise and undesirable to attempt to regulate every hour of the student's time while he is in college. Freedom, as well as responsibility, should be encouraged on every campus. One never learns to swim by keeping away from the water. The individual never learns to live on a rational plane without ample opportunity for independent action. But just as one learns to swim by learning the effectiveness of the different strokes, so the adolescent youth learns to live most effectively through directed experience. It is only by this means that the inexperienced student can acquire assurance and confidence in his practices.

Dualism in learning, as I see it, consists in using all the

experiences of college life in the interest of better standards of living. Training for a profession is inadequate if it does not do more for the individual than to place him in possession of the tools with which he is to make a living. Even training in professional ethics is not sufficient. I have known doctors who had a high sense of their professional relations with other doctors but who were not honest in their personal dealings with their patients. I have known lawyers who were highly honorable in their dealings with other lawyers but who were not equally scrupulous with their clients. Professional training of every character must do more for the student than this. It must impart to him a high sense of honor in all his relationships—professional and otherwise—to the end that he will go out into the world to make a success in his profession and dignify it by right conduct and right ideals in all the relations of life.

There is not a single subject offered for formal instruction that does not give opportunity for educating the whole man. It is possible to teach ethics in a thousand ways without referring to the subject. Every professor, for example, who insists on thorough preparation is developing unconsciously in the student a sense of responsibility. On the other hand, every instructor who allows his students to do shoddy work is encouraging superficiality. Integrity in education while recognizing the dualism in learning means in its finality that the whole man must understand the unity of purpose running through the entire educational process.

I come to you, therefore, again to emphasize the seriousness of the task you are entering upon in this new year. A college education cannot be acquired without serious work. There are hardships, anxieties, and sometimes heart-burnings to be experienced in the acquisition of knowledge. The cost is high. The rewards are very great to those who are willing to pay the price. I admonish you to keep your thoughts on the main thing. Your first obligation and your first concern should be to get things in their right relations here. See to it that day after day you give first place to the supreme purpose of getting a well-rounded education, and regard all else as incidental. There are many incidental things in college life that are important, but they are not supremely important. There is a place for pleasant associations, for many forms of recreation, and they are not to be despised; but they are secondary to the serious purpose of learning to live and learning to make a living.

I desire above all else that the University of Oklahoma may be known far and wide as a place where learning is fostered, where mental health is united with sound scholarship, and where genuine culture is diffused with high character. I would have you become what Xenophon described Socrates as being—a man "so pious that he did nothing without the sanctions of the gods; so just, that he wronged no man even in the most trifling affair; so temperate that he never preferred pleasure to virtue; so wise, that he never erred in distinguishing better from worse; so capable of discerning the character of others, of confuting those who were in error, and of exhorting them to virtue and honor, he seemed to be such as the best and happiest of men would be." This is the ideal I set up for the university and for you. The university becomes your foster mother today. As you enter upon the year's work, I would voice the prayer of the university for you in the words of Hector to his sons, slightly paraphrased: "O God, grant that these, my children, may do good and bear noble rule. May their mother be glad at heart."

THE CHANGING STATE UNIVERSITY[1]

CHAPTER TWELVE

EDUCATIONAL institutions of every grade and character are undergoing important changes at the present time. Many of these changes reflect radical departures from established organization and policy. Dissatisfaction with educational accomplishment, as well as economic necessity, accounts for this situation. While the most spectacular changes are taking place in the institutions of higher learning, the same influences are at work in the primary, secondary, and even the private schools below the college level.

It goes without saying that not all these changes are desirable. Economic necessity has forced both colleges and secondary schools to restrict their academic programs, to reduce personnel, and to make other adjustments that will certainly retard the progress of education. But, undoubtedly, the searching of hearts that financial distress has brought to education will produce some beneficial results. To what extent the losses will be offset by gains is impossible to determine at this time. The historians of the future will certainly find that many foolish things have been said and done. Let us hope that some of these may be offset by words and deeds that may have been wise and constructive.

The state universities, like all other educational institu-

1. Reproduced from *The University of Chicago Magazine* for March, 1934.

tions, are in process of readjustment. Changes are taking place in this group of institutions that will profoundly influence educational thought and accomplishment for all time to come. Most of the changes are the result of necessity created by financial adversity; but some have come in response to changing political, economic, and social conditions. The state universities, as functional agencies of society, have been quite responsive to changing conditions throughout their history. In the past, however, these changes have been evolutionary. Today, they have a tendency to become revolutionary.

The state universities have been exerting an increasing influence upon the cultural life of America through several generations. These institutions were not established simultaneously. The number has been slowly increasing for more than a hundred years. The idea of providing higher education at state expense originated in the political and social liberalism that developed in America during the latter part of the eighteenth century. The ideas of equality of opportunity and freedom within the law were uppermost in the thoughts of men in that creative age. Education appeared to thoughtful men as the most direct means of securing these blessings to all mankind. George Washington shared the views of his contemporaries concerning the importance of education as an agency of the new social order. Leonard C. Helderman, in his *George Washington: Patron of Learning*, states that Washington had the idea of a national university at the time he took command of the Continental Army under the Cambridge Elm in 1775. Correspondence with men of his day supports this assertion. The fact that he discussed the subject in both his first and last messages to Congress shows how seriously he regarded the matter. Washington's views were certainly in harmony with the liberal thought of his times.

The dream of Washington and other statesmen of his day has never been realized, although the policy of establishing a national university has been under consideration from time to time ever since the establishment of our national government. His views concerning education took deep root in the minds of men throughout the country. An institution that evolved into a state university was established in Georgia in 1784, and a similar institution was established in North Carolina in 1789—the year that our national government was organized. It will be recalled that only five universities in this country antedate the establishment of these two institutions—Harvard, Yale, Pennsylvania, Princeton, and Columbia (King's College). It is a matter of great significance that the state university came early in our history and helped to give impulse and direction to higher education throughout the nation.

The nineteenth century was pre-eminently the century of educational advancement. Educational history has no parallel to it in any time or country. The number of colleges and universities multiplied rapidly during this century. The number of students increased slowly at first but gained increasing momentum through the years. The physical facilities for higher education increased with the growth of population and the development of our natural resources. The state university movement reflected all these influences.

The University of Virginia was founded by Thomas Jefferson in 1819, the University of Michigan in 1841, and the University of Wisconsin in 1849. A great impulse was given to state-supported institutions of higher learning by the passage of the Morrill Act in 1862, for out of the land grants authorized by this act many of the great state universities have grown. Today there are forty-nine state universities, including the territorial institutions in Hawaii, the Philippines, and Porto Rico. It happens that in the state of Ohio there are three state-supported universities. There is a state university today in all but four of the states of the Union.

The state university differs in origin and, in some respects, in objective from the private universities. As educational agencies of the several states, they have their functions prescribed by constitutional provisions and legislative enactments. All of these institutions are obligated to provide instruction in many fields of learning to resident students, to conduct research, and to provide educational opportunities for adults throughout the states in which they are located. Every publicly supported university is expected to inculcate state pride on the part of students in the traditions and history of the state and to disseminate our cultural heritage throughout the population.

Professional education is a recognized function of the state university. High standards in professional training have been maintained in these institutions for a long time. Of course, the state university shares the responsibility of academic instruction and professional training with all of the great private universities; but the justification for technical training at state expense is based upon the theory that those receiving this training will assume leadership and render some public service independent of professional obligation. From time to time there has been opposition to the establishment of professional schools in these institutions on the ground that the state is not obligated to provide a professional education to anyone. In answer to this objection, two arguments have been advanced. In the first place, it is contended that professional training is inherent in the idea of a university; and, in the second place, the policy has been defended on the theory that the state should provide leaders in the professions of law, medicine, pharmacy, dentistry, engineering, journalism, etc., as a means of providing an adequate number of men of professional qualifications in the several fields who are willing to render public service independent of their professions. There is no question that the private universities attempt to do the same thing. I admit there is not much evidence to support the theory that the professional graduate of the state university reveals more passion for public service than similar graduates from private universities, but it is undoubtedly true that professional training at state expense is largely to be justified on this theory.

Most of the functions to which reference has been made are inherent in every university worthy of the name, but the state university is charged with other obligations not generally assumed by private universities. The state university is essentially an agency of social welfare. As such, it is expected to perform many educational services that are not usually performed by other types of universities. These functions have been disparaged by some, and ridiculed by others. M. Maurice Caullery, a professor at the Sorbonne and a former exchange professor of Harvard, in a survey of higher education in the United States, says: "Through their origin, the state universities have had at the beginning some very utilitarian tendencies. They have, before all else, striven for practical application and teaching. Real culture has only little by little made a place for itself in them, and is still often rather cramped, and much of the teaching smacks of the soil."

The state universities freely admit that they strive for practical application, both in their teaching and research functions. Their friends, however, do not agree that "real culture has only little by little made a place for itself in them." They vigorously deny that their practical objectives have cramped their cultural functions. They boast of many scientific discoveries that have contributed to the wealth and happiness of the American people.

The attitude of the state universities toward educational

[151]

service was forcibly stated by President Lotus D. Coffman, of the University of Minnesota, in an address at the Conference of Universities held under the auspices of New York University in 1932. He said: "The state universities hold that there is no intellectual service too undignified for them to perform. They maintain that every time they lift the intellectual level of any class or group, they enhance the intellectual opportunities of every other class or group. They maintain that every time they teach any group or class the importance of relying upon tested information as the basis for action, they advance the cause of science. They maintain that every time they teach any class or group in society how to live better, to read more and to read more discriminatingly, to do any of the things that stimulate intellectual or esthetic interest and effort, they thereby enlarge the group's outlook on life, make its members more cosmopolitan in their points of view, and improve their standard of living. These are services which no state university would shrink from performing."

It is this larger obligation of the state university to the social order that has made it sensitive to changing social conditions. The increasing complexity of organized society and the multiplication of problems resulting from this situation have given to the state university its greatest opportunity. It has made continuous adjustments, both in organization and objectives, in an effort to fulfill its high mission.

In these recent years, the state universities have been experiencing critical revaluation. There has been a reappraisal of both structure and procedure. In fact, every function of government has been subject to this process as a result of the necessity for rigid economy. The state universities of the country, without exception, have been compelled to practice unforeseen economies in order to survive. This situation has brought serious problems to governing

[152]

boards and administrative officers—problems that are new and difficult of solution. Before the "years of the locust," to use a phrase of Mr. Gilbert Seldes in describing the period of the depression, state universities were increasing their facilities rapidly. Increasing enrolment called for larger faculties, more and better equipment, and new buildings. The public was making new demands upon these institutions for all kinds of public service. The state governments were reasonably responsive to these demands. Public revenues were supplied in continuously increasing amounts in each recurring biennium until the collapse came. Those of us who had been guiding these institutions in high gear found ourselves compelled to shift to neutral about 1930; and then as taxable revenues collapsed, we found it necessary to go into reverse. Educational administrators had no experience in running the educational machine backwards. It was not easy to keep the machine in the road. It was not surprising that some of us found ourselves off the road on dangerous curves or getting off the pavement where the soil was soft and the driving difficult. The situation called for courage, ingenuity, and sometimes quick action.

In common with all other educational institutions, it became necessary to reduce salaries. These reductions have ranged from ten to fifty per cent. The public will never know what this did to the morale of faculty members and other employees; but everyone recognized the necessity for this action and, in general, it was accepted philosophically. It became necessary to curtail, or to discontinue, all building programs; even repairs and campus improvements were discontinued. All these things were necessary to keep expenditures within budget allowances. These drastic measures, however, have not satisfied public demand for economy. State budget committees and tax officials have demanded co-ordination of effort and the elimination of needless duplication in many state-supported institutions of

[153]

higher learning. When times were prosperous, many states increased unnecessarily the number of their state-supported educational institutions. In some cases these institutions were established out of a sincere desire to provide adequate educational facilities for the people; but, in many instances, these institutions were created as the result of patronage. It was inevitable that the time should come when the several states would not be able to support all the institutions that they had established. In fact, many of them have never been adequately supported.

Some of these institutions have rendered good service to the cause of education, but many tax-supported institutions have been overambitious and expanded their teaching programs by upgrading or otherwise as a means of increasing their enrolments. Quality in education has been sacrificed to a quantitative standard. This situation has discredited the work of the universities and impaired their usefulness.

This unfortunate situation has been going on for a long time. The public has been dissatisfied with educational results. Social pressure has forced a thorough re-appraisal of values and accomplishment. State-supported institutions have been compelled to undertake vast experiments and to undergo close scrutiny. These things have been justified on grounds of economy and efficiency. Survey commissions have been busily collecting data and formulating policies. The most recent of these have been made in Oregon, California, Georgia, North Carolina, Oklahoma and Texas. The plans of co-ordination that have been proposed in the several states are not equally promising of beneficial results. The thorough reorganization of the educational system in Oregon, for example, does not give promise at the present time of advancing the cause of higher education. On the other hand, constructive results seem assured from the Georgia and North Carolina plans. The efforts to co-ordinate both state-supported and private colleges in Oklahoma are progressing slowly, but the problems are difficult and it is not possible to predict what will result from the undertaking. Far-reaching plans for the co-ordination of the tax-supported institutions in Texas were proposed last year; but the situation in Texas is complicated, due to the vast area of the state and the unusually large number of state-supported institutions. What the final results will be no one can predict at the present time.

How will the state universities be affected by these various plans for co-ordination? This question is not easy to answer. Public sentiment and educational rivalry are variable factors in this whole situation. In some of the states where serious proposals for elimination of duplication through co-ordination are under way, the state university is regarded as just one institution very much like all other institutions, regardless of its educational importance. In other states, of course, the state university is recognized as the head of the educational system of the state and the general public appreciates the large service it is rendering to the cause of education.

Internal, as well as external, co-ordination is equally imperative under existing conditions. A rapid examination of the curricula in state universities is under way in several of these institutions. There is a widespread belief that all universities have multiplied their courses and increased their personnel unduly. Every head of a department has been anxious to increase his personnel. The only means of doing this has been by fractionalizing the content of the courses in the department. This has greatly increased the overhead cost and unnecessarily reduced the content of courses. A new synthesis, both of departments and courses, is demanded by every consideration of educational policy and economic necessity. This situation presents a difficult problem for administrative officers and governing boards, for this process involves the demotion of some department heads and the reduction of the teaching personnel. It will require courage and tact of a high order; but, undoubtedly, in the years immediately ahead, we will see a much simpler organization in our colleges and universities and a complete breakdown in the air-tight compartments of learning.

The state universities have been compelled to take account of the junior college movement. The number of junior colleges is increasing and all senior colleges and universities must give consideration to the place they are to occupy in the scheme of education. Will the junior college ultimately replace the first two years of undergraduate work in both private and state-supported universities? This question is being raised frequently these days and educators are not of the same mind with reference to the answer. I, personally, do not believe that the junior college will eliminate the freshman and sophomore years in the state universities; but it seems certain that it will bring about the reorganization of undergraduate work. It seems now that the liberal arts colleges will be divided into junior and senior divisions. In fact, several experiments of this kind are under way at the present time. It may be that the time will come when the university proper will begin at the junior year and all graduate and professional courses will begin above the junior college level. The junior college movement seems to make this policy necessary; but, for practical reasons, it will be necessary for the state universities to maintain the first two years of the college course as a basis for the senior, graduate, and professional school work.

Finally, the problem of student enrolment is calling for serious consideration. There is a general belief that far too many students are entering our colleges and universities.

This belief has been held for a long time. Carlyle said in *Sartor Resartus:* "Among eleven hundred Christian youths, some eleven are eager to learn." Many people share Carlyle's belief today, varying only the percentages in the analysis. Should people be taxed to provide educational facilities for young men and women who are unable to profit by educational advantages or are indifferent to their opportunities? The answer is "No." It is believed that some method should be devised to eliminate the unfit and indifferent before they enter college. Intelligence tests have been applied without very satisfactory results. Entrance examinations have been proposed and, in a few places, this is the method adopted for admission to college. But students continue to enrol in our colleges and universities in increasing numbers and this may continue as long as high schools graduate increasing numbers of boys and girls. It is probably true, however, that state universities are rapidly reaching their maximum enrolments. Junior colleges will divert large numbers from universities for the first two years and more accurate measures of student capacities will be devised to separate the intellectual sheep from the moronistic goats. Certainly, the trend is toward quality in education rather than quantity; and every university worthy of the name must devise methods to accomplish this result.

The widespread belief that the dissemination of knowledge is a public obligation and that training for leadership is a just charge upon the taxpayer seems to justify a prophecy. The state university will survive the cataclysms that occur from time to time, just as Bologna, Paris, Oxford, Vienna, and Heidelberg have survived them. Future generations will recognize that the state university was one of the great contributions that the nineteenth century made to our civilization. These state-supported institutions will continue to exert a large influence upon the intellectual life of the nation. Their usefulness will increase or decline from time to time with changing political fortunes and economic conditions. They will always be peculiarly sensitive to social demand and political expediency, but the possibility of the survival of our state universities is not one of the uncertain factors in our national program of education.

QUALITY IN LEARNING[1]

CHAPTER THIRTEEN

THE AGE in which we live is characterized by quantitative rather than qualitative standards. We think in terms of bigness. Mass production dominates our thinking. John Ruskin, more than a century ago, challenged this philosophy when he said: "Every man should do good work for his bread; secondly, every man should have good bread for his work." He defines political economy as being "the multiplication of human life at the highest standard." To his way of thinking, "the entire object of true education is to make people not merely *do* the right things, but *enjoy* the right things: not merely industrious, but to love industry— not merely learned, but to love knowledge—not merely pure, but to love purity—not merely just, but to hunger and thirst after justice." No one, perhaps, has ever stated the ideals of education more accurately than Ruskin has in this far-reaching statement. But where is there to be found an educational institution or a school system that approximates in its accomplishments this comprehensive goal? The time has come, however, when education, like all the other aspects of life, must be measured by qualitative rather than quantitative standards.

We do not realize how imperfectly we measure the standards of our civilization when we speak in terms of quanti-

1. Address delivered at the Honors Day exercises, Iowa State College, Ames, Iowa, May 24, 1934.

[159]

tative values. We recall with pride, for example, the vast area of the United States, the growth in population, and the size of our factories and their annual output. But the area of Canada is larger than that of the United States, and Russia has more people within its confines than we have in this country. The productive resources of the United States far surpass those of Canada, and the high percentage of illiteracy in Russia has retarded the progress of that country for centuries.

Mass production in ideas may be as inadequate in measuring the standards of civilization as mass production is in measuring industrial output. We boast of the enormous increase in our public school facilities. We find a great deal of satisfaction in reporting from year to year that the enrolment of students in our high schools, colleges, and universities exceeds that of preceding years. The number of our colleges, universities, and technical schools in the United States has increased greatly since the beginning of this century. But what about the quality of instruction? Have the standards of education been raised? Are we making more efficient use of the educational facilities that have been placed at our disposal? These are questions that must be answered before the public will know very much about educational accomplishment.

It is quite evident today that the American people are not satisfied with the quantitative standards in education. Critical-mindedness has taken the place of a blind acceptance of things as they are in our thinking. Skepticism about social values and objectives is reflected in platform utterances and editorial expression. The age in which we live is one of disillusionment. The World War jarred us loose from an attitude of complacence and a false sense of security. There is no institution of society that is free today from attack. The searchlight of critical opinion is being focused squarely upon the home, church, school and government.

This state of mind has its values as well as its perils. Complacence is not desirable in a dynamic social order. Institutions, after all, are functional agencies of society. They need to readjust both their objectives and their practices from time to time, if they are to serve social needs effectively. But there is always danger, in times like these, that the good will be sacrificed with the bad. There is danger that because imperfections are found in the working of our social agencies the people may completely lose faith in them. There is no greater responsibility confronting us today than that of differentiating between the values that should be conserved and the practices that should be discarded. The only way out of this difficulty is through a more discriminating attitude on the part of those who direct our social agencies. Educators, of all people in our society, should possess this attribute. They should define their methods of appraisal in terms of actual accomplishment. This is the only means by which we can win back the confidence of the public in the things we are attempting to do.

The defects in education are essentially the defects of our social order. The problems of society at large have been reflected in our school system. The increase in population, the drift of people from rural to urban communities, and the substitution of factory production in industry for the apprentice system have changed both the conditions and the habits of living. The industrial revolution produced the machine, and the machine ushered in the power age. These changes have influenced our thinking in many ways. Our public school system developed in an agrarian society. It has had to function for fifty years in a highly industrialized environment. It is not surprising that our schools from time to time have gotten out of step with the society in which they are expected to function. On the other hand, it

[161]

is rather surprising that our school system has been able to make so many timely adjustments in an effort to serve more effectively those for whom its benefits were designed.

No one can truthfully contend that our schools have remained static in a dynamic age. The fact is, there is no other institution in our society that has been more sensitive to social change. The content of courses has been constantly revised, teaching methods have been improved, and the structural organization has been adjusted repeatedly in an effort to keep pace with the influences about them.

As evidence of this fact, I remind you that in the decade following the Civil War the best in the educational experience of the leading countries of Europe was freely incorporated into our school system. Free-hand drawing was borrowed from England. We adopted manual training as practised in the Russian schools, and the kindergarten was adapted from its Germanic origin. As our industrial organization increased in complexity, vocational subjects were included in the high-school curriculum. The expansion of the courses of study created a very complicated problem. It became apparent that the growing child could not do all the work that the enlarged program contemplated within the time allotted for high-school instruction. These changes produced serious difficulties for our colleges and universities. The old classical curriculum, based on a fixed schedule of studies, could not be maintained. There was but one way out of the difficulty, and that was through the elective system. President Charles W. Eliot of Harvard is given credit for this innovation; but it was inevitable, under the pressure of circumstances, that an elective system should develop and parallel courses at high-school and college levels should be inaugurated. All of these changes were made in an effort to better serve the needs of a new kind of social situation. In the light of the perspective that we now have, it was quite apparent that thoroughness was sacrificed to expediency. Much of the new subject matter that was incorporated in the curricula was thin in content. There was no body of knowledge of adequate porportions to sustain the courses. In the course of time, some of these subjects acquired a body of knowledge through scientific investigation; but no one can gainsay that the sacrifice of the old disciplinary subjects resulted in superficiality.

The conditions of life during the past half century have produced an endless conflict between qualitative and quantitative values. Mass production in industry has often sacrificed quality to quantity. Demand for goods increased with the growth in population. The population doubled every twenty years between 1790 and 1850. It has doubled twice since that time. The history of machine production is little more than an effort of organized society to supply this rapidly increasing population with the things it demanded for sustaining life and providing physical comforts. The ends may have justified the means. The industrial efficiency of American producers has attracted the favorable attention of the world, but there is no denying the fact that much of the output of manufactured goods has been shoddy and inferior in quality to that produced under the apprentice system.

Mass production in education has had a similar history. Demands upon the schools also increased with the growth in population. The enrolment has reflected the increase in population. Expenditures for school facilities, including buildings and equipment, have been unprecedented. It has been increasingly difficult to provide the schools with an adequate number of well qualified teachers. This is true of the primary and secondary schools, as well as the colleges and universities. Our schools have produced enormously, but there has been an increasing dissatisfaction with the quality of our products.

[163]

Every primary pupil today expects to continue through high school, and every high-school graduate is a potential college student. The number of graduates from our high schools is approximately equal to the total enrolment in high schools a generation ago, and the number of students completing college courses today about equals the total enrolment of the colleges a half century ago. There was a time when students coming up to college thought of themselves as the favored few. Today the college student takes his enrolment in an institution of higher learning as a matter of course. As a consequence, many students enter our colleges and universities with no love for learning and without much intellectual interest in the subjects they are required to take. The result is that there is little connection between education and scholarship. A college diploma is not a very accurate measure of intellectual accomplishment. All that it signifies is that a student has spent four years in some institution of higher learning and acquired one hundred and twenty or more hours of credit in the subject matter of a curriculum.

The number of demands that are being made upon the students' time has increased enormously in recent years. This situation presents almost insuperable problems to educators. A generation or more ago, every student came to college for the primary purpose of acquiring an education. There were few outside interests to distract his attention, but the situation is quite different today. This topic is the subject of almost every educational convention; but, as Mark Twain commented on the weather, little is being done about the matter.

The increase in the number of so-called "extra-curricular activities" is largely the result of mass education. These activities multiplied as an increasing number of young people enrolled in schools and colleges who were not primarily interested in learning. There was need of an outlet for their energies and it was found in athletics, fraternities, social amusements, student politics, and numerous other energy-consuming agencies. As early as 1909, Woodrow Wilson, writing in *Scribner's Magazine*, complained that "the side shows are so numerous, so diverting—so important, if you will—that they have swallowed up the circus, and those who perform in the main tent must often whistle for their audiences, discouraged and humiliated." But "the side shows" were relatively few in Wilson's day compared with the number at present.

There is no question that some of the extra-curricular activities of students have educational value. Some of them help the student to find himself, to measure his ability, and to co-ordinate his efforts. Much of the leadership that appears in the social and political life of the nation had its origin in some of these organizations. It is equally certain, however, that some of these activities are incompatible with scholarly habits and detrimental to sound learning. It is not easy for the average student to differentiate between them. Few students are wise enough to budget their time in such a way as to get the most out of their college experience. The result is that in too many cases energy is dissipated and preparation for classroom instruction is neglected.

I am making no plea for a return to the old order of things. College life is more enjoyable than it was in my youth. I am glad of it. But when one attempts to balance the gains against the losses, there is no question that scholarship is being sacrificed. I very much fear that we compromise in many instances the quality of learning in order to make a Roman holiday for the enormous number of students who find little satisfaction in the exacting requirements of the educational process. Few of us would like

[165]

to admit that we are providing many students with entertainment when we should be disseminating knowledge.

I am convinced that a simpler college environment is necessary, if we are to conserve our educational ideals. Many of our students are dissatisfied with their own accomplishments after four years of college residence. They come up to their graduation today with a sense of disillusionment. They feel that there is something spurious about a college degree. No one today knows how to evaluate a diploma. It no longer gives a genuine sense of satisfaction to graduate from college. No one today knows what a college degree represents because the range of intellectual accomplishment varies between such wide limits.

The competition between curricular and extra-curricular activities of students has caused educators to resort to all kinds of expedients in an effort to maintain satisfactory standards. The various systems of grading, as practiced in our colleges and universities, are designed to measure educational results. How inadequately they accomplish the purpose is well known to every teacher. It is one of the travesties of education that colleges and universities are compelled to require students to attend classes. Several of our educational institutions have experimented with the voluntary plan, but the results have not been very satisfactory. Unless there is intellectual tradition behind the student and a genuine desire for knowledge, as well as scholarly teachers who are able to make the subject matter of instruction interesting, voluntary class attendance cannot be made successful. These highly desirable conditions do not prevail in many of our colleges and universities today.

But even under the compulsory policy of class attendance and strict limitation on class "cuts," it has been necessary to set up other safeguards. The student today is not only required to pass his courses, but he is expected to accumulate a certain number of grade points as well. This is merely a device to improve the quality of the student's work. As we say in academic parlance, it is designed to improve the student's general average. As paradoxical as it may appear, a student may pass all his courses in a four-year curriculum and fail to accumulate a sufficient number of grade points to graduate. This appears quite absurd to many parents; but without some plan of weighting the grades of many students, the level of educational accomplishment would settle down to an embarrassingly low level.

The grade-point system is so generally practiced today that most of us have forgotten the conditions that brought it into educational practice. But the fact is that it reflects the educator's strategy in the competition with extra-curricular activities. It is the challenge to the student who holds that a gentleman's grade should not be above "C."

I hesitate to criticize a system that is so generally believed in by educational officials. I confess that I have had a part in its development. It is quite apparent, however, that the whole system of measuring educational results is quite artificial. It is equally apparent that it has added greatly to the mechanics of education. If you doubt my statement, visit the registrar's office in any one of our larger colleges and universities. When I was in college, the registrar's office was a small alcove in one of the buildings and the student records that were kept there were very simple—perhaps too simple and rather inadequate. But today the registrar's office is an elaborate counting-house. The registrar is a statistician, as well as an educator. His offices are filled with experts who are specialists in some aspect of personnel work. The floor space is covered with cabinets filled with thousands of cards relating to all kinds of information about students and their work. These records are the refuge of the deans and the pride of the president.

But I am wondering whether or not this elaborate

[167]

machinery does not imply that there is something wrong with educational practice. Why should it be necessary to keep this elaborate check on the student's progress through college? After all, learning is more than acquiring knowledge. Learning, as Ruskin states, is a love of knowledge and a passion for truth. For those who possess these qualities, there is no mechanical device that can measure accomplishment.

I am not advocating the abolishment of credit hours, required courses, grade points, and all the other contrivances that modern education has devised; but I am calling attention to the time and money consumed by the mechanics of educational procedure. Education is a matter of mental attitudes, and mechanical devices have little to do with it.

There is a definite relationship between the mechanics of education and the quality of teaching. The use of artificial incentives to study indicates that those intrusted with intellectual guidance are not highly successful. Henry Clay Trumbull once said: "Unless something has been learned, nothing has been taught." The soundness of this philosophy cannot be questioned; but in the light of it, there are many teachers who are holding classes rather than instructing students. There are too many instructors who think they have fully performed their duty to their students when they have exposed them to a body of knowledge. It is this attitude on the part of teachers that makes artificial stimuli, such as credit hours, grade points and similar devices, necessary in our educational practice.

Charles A. Dana once told the sudents of Union College that there were three essentials to education:

"First, that one shall see what he looks at, in all its qualities, distinctions, perspectives, and relations, and be able to think about it intelligently.

[168]

"Second, that he shall be able to communicate his vision and his thoughts about it with accuracy, force, and grace.

"Third, that he shall know how to find out what he needs to know, being able to locate and depend exclusively upon the reliable sources of information."

There is no such thing as good teaching that does not recognize these essentials. Students must be taught to see things in their right relations. They must be able to communicate what they know clearly and accurately. It is equally important for every student to learn the sources of knowledge. It is not expected, of course, that all this can be accomplished in a short time; but every one who attempts to guide the intellectual interests of students should keep these essentials in mind, and no student should be recommended for graduation who has not acquired these habits of thought.

There is a widespread belief among educators that the quality of teaching is much better in our high schools than in our colleges. This, of course, is a debatable question. There is a vast amount of poor instruction in both high schools and colleges. Educational administrators are usually very much concerned about the scholarship of those invited to membership on their faculties. Knowledge alone, however, does not insure good instruction. Good teaching involves not only a knowledge of the subject matter to be taught, but enthusiasm and ability to impart knowledge to others.

There are many good teachers in our educational institutions, and a few great ones. But candor compels me to admit there are some that are incompetent or indifferent. Qualities of mind and heart vary too much between individuals to expect any one faculty to be composed entirely of good instructors. The ability to impart knowledge is a great art. As I look back over my college days, I can recall but few teachers who had the ability to fire their students with

[169]

enthusiasm and challenge them to their best efforts. A similar situation prevails in our educational institutions today. But it will be impossible to improve greatly the quality of learning unless we can find a way to increase the number of teachers who are genuinely devoted to their tasks and who have a passion for learning.

Many a student can say of his instructors what Tennyson said of some of his teachers at Trinity College, Cambridge:

". . . You who do profess to teach,
And teach us nothing, feeding not the heart!"

I have been convinced for a long time that something should be done to improve the quality of college instruction. High-school instruction has been improved by careful supervision. I am fully aware that college men and women are very much opposed to supervision of their work; but I am sure that we will never greatly improve college teaching until a system of supervision, based on sound methods of instruction, is put into effect.

All that I have said implies that popular education remains very much of an experiment. We still do not know how far it is possible to extend knowledge. There are those who believe that educational accomplishment is decreased in proportion as its benefits are enlarged. There is no greater problem in a democratic society like ours than that of setting metes and bounds to educational opportunity.

The recognition of intellectual differences implies that terminal levels of learning must be devised for everyone who seeks an education. Little has been done in this direction up to the present time. Educational tests and measurements remain a clumsy instrument in our hands. Our practices would indicate that we believe every child has

[170]

an unlimited capacity to acquire knowledge, to succeed in any profession to which he may aspire, become a grand opera singer, paint like Raphael or Leonardo da Vinci, or write poetry like Wordsworth or Whittier. That tragedy should result from this laissez faire policy is not surprising to anyone who surveys the situation.

Our educational institutions have shown a strange indifference to the quality of its student material. Colleges and universities still complacently assume that fifteen high school credits constitute all that is necessary for a student to assimilate profitably the subject matter of a college curriculum. That this admission formula is inadequate is known to educators everywhere, but little is being done about it.

If we get on successfully in the future, the instructor must give a new interpretation to *instruere*. He must study the student, as well as the subject matter of his courses. Genuine thought must be given to capacities, possibilities, and adaptable materials. As the student comes to occupy a larger place in the processes of learning, the curriculum should more and more become the background of his interests. When this is done, the desiccated elements of learning, reflected in terms of credit hours, grade points and similar devices, will gradually lose their validity. It is certain that until students learn to grapple for themselves with the actual content of subject matter, they will not get satisfaction out of their educational experience.

I am wondering what would happen if some college or university should have the courage to say to its freshman class as it enters upon its work: "All the resources of this institution are placed at your disposal, including the time of every faculty member. We make no requirements of you, except that you will conform to good standards of conduct and demonstrate that you have ability to profit by your environment. But we reserve the right at frequent intervals

[171]

to test your progress and to measure your accomplishment. If at any time you do not show that you are making reasonable progress, your connection with the institution will be promptly severed. After a reasonable length of time, should you reveal that your actual knowledge is adequate, a diploma will be awarded to you."

I confess I know of no institution that would dare to make this experiment; but this, after all, is the goal toward which we are striving. I, personally, do not believe that it is impossible of realization in the future. If the time should ever come when we could substitute qualitative for quantitative ideals in education, it would be possible to eliminate much of the mechanics connected with the educational process. We might not be able completely to do away with credits, grade points, semester hours and the like; but we could restore to education the satisfaction of regarding it as an achievement—a feeling of mastery in the conquest of knowledge. This is the task ahead. To it we should dedicate our best endeavors.

FINIS

INDEX

functional agencies of society, 122; trouble with, 126; attitude of instructors in, 143, 168; changes taking place in, 147; increase in, 148, 160; establishment of, 149; problem of enrolment is, 156; best in schools of Europe adopted in our, 162; registrar's office in, 167; poor instruction in, 169; means to insure better instruction in, 170; admission to, 171; suggested experiment for students entering, 172.

College spirit, meaning of, 41.

College students: interest of, 25; contrast of, today with those of former days, 36; divided loyalties of, 40; wide range in intellectual outlook of, 45; moral code for, 47; proper perspective necessary for, 47; habits of work, 48; two worlds open to, 59; prophecy for, 61, 62; questions to be asked of, 66, 80; preparation of, 68; imparting knowledge to, 68; environment forty years ago of, 72; high tension of, 73; choices to be made by, 77, 84; what they have a right to expect, 88, 89; homesickness among, 93; financial needs of, 94; limited resources of, 104; quality of work measured by use made of leisure time by, 125; supreme task of, 133; hours of preparation for classroom work of, 143, 144; attitude of, today, 164; demands made upon time of, 164; compulsory class attendance for, 166; devices to improve quality of work of, 166, 167, 168; many dissatisfied with results, 166.

Committee on Intellectual Co-operation, 16.

Cornell, Ezra, ideal for university of, 120.

Crane, Dr. Frank, quoted, 62.

Crothers, Samuel McChord, quoted, 49.

Dana, Charles A., address of, 26, 168.

Davidson, Thomas, on the aim of education, 4.

da Vinci, Leonardo, contribution of, 127.

Dental education, needs of, 13.

Depression: hardships caused by, 94; remedies for, 96, 97; solution of unemployment problem in, 98, 99; graduation during, 118.

Dewey, John, quoted, 52.

Dimnet, Abbé Ernest, quoted, 69.

Diploma, evaluation of, 166.

Durant, Will, quoted, 107.

Education: objectives of, 4, 26, 28; instruction and research in, 5; obligation to supply trained leadership, 11; character results of, 14; advancement of, 16; charges against, 17; selective processes of, 22, 23; no free, 26; three essentials to, 26, 168; aim of, 27; lack of interest of students in, 28; fulfillment of promises in, 29; per capita cost of, 32; in America, 37; two explanations for failure in, 38; unbalanced attitude toward institution in, 39; professional training in, 39; dualism in, 42, 142; common interest in religion and, 46; cure for social ills, 49; false connotations of, 49; blame for dullness in, 60; influence of, 62; two problems of, 63; paradoxes in, 84, 85, 86; procrastination in, 85; preparation for effective living, 88; value of, 97; retrenchment in, 95, 153; debt of maturity to youth is, 98; perils involved in, 109, 110; concerned with achievement, 114; self-evaluation is object of, 115; conflict of individualism and collectivism in, 119, 120; theories of Montaigne and Rousseau on, 120; limitations on, 121; for leisure, 124; development of whole man is task of, 126; two schools of thought in, 133, 134; designed to adapt one to his environment, 136; integrity in, 145; quality sacrificed to quantity in, 154; mass production in, 159, 163; quantitative standards in, 160; defects of, 161; mechanics of, 166, 167, 168; popular, an experiment, 170.

Einstein, Albert, theories advanced by, 55.

Lindbergh, Charles A., aërial flights of, 56, 91.

Literature: less being read, 74; outlines of, 74; tendencies in, 74; reflection of machines in, 75; masterpieces being read less, 75.

Lowell, A. Lawrence, on American education, 28.

Loyalties, value of, 40, 41.

Luther, Martin, quoted, 137.

Martin, Everett Dean, on the meaning of a liberal education, 46, 50.

Meiklejohn, Dr. Alexander, inaugural address of, 27, 28.

Mendel, contribution of, 128.

Millikan, Robert A., investigations of, 56.

Milton, John, quoted, 4.

Monnet, Julien C., 4.

Montaigne, theory of education of, 120.

Morand, Paul, quoted, 72.

Munro, William Bennett, quoted, 63, 64.

National university, views of Washington on, 148.

Newman, Cardinal John Henry, quoted, 81, 82.

Newton, Sir Isaac, experiments of, 55.

New York Times, quoted, 97, 124.

NRA: collectivism in business under, 121; industrial codes of, 122, 124; criticism of, 130.

Oklahoma, Territory of, 3, 103.

Oklahoma, University of: former presidents of, 3; founding of, 3; growth of, 3, 18; contributions that should be made by, 10; obligations of, 10; graduate school of, 12; medical education in, 13; extension teaching, 14; location of, 16, 73; every element of population enrolled in, 28; growth of enrolment in, 29; purposes for all effort in, 34; boundaries of campus of, 44; enrolment in, 44, 67, 81; admonition to students in, 45; number completing degrees in, 45, 118; teachers in, 67; "no-car rule" at, 73; prob-

lems affecting the, 103; policy of retrenchment in, 104; equation in all courses in, 114; one of beauty spots of Oklahoma, 114; critical year in history of, 116; ideal for, 146.

Oklahoma, mineral resources of, 8.

Oklahoma City Times, quoted, 62.

Ordinance of 1787, educational provisions of, 4.

Outlines, day of, 74.

Pasteur, Louis, research of, 55.

Peabody, Francis G., quoted, 80.

Piccard, Auguste, balloon ascension of, 91.

Pitkin, Walter B., on use of time, 126.

Plato, story of Dionysius, 77.

Polando, John, exploits in air of, 91.

Polite Unlearning, the Anglo-American School of, 51.

Post, Wiley, exploits in air of, 91.

Priestley, contribution of, 128.

Professional training, 39, 150.

Professorships, exchange of, 16.

Proverbs, quotation from, 33.

Psychology, needs for, 106.

Public officials, integrity of, 12, 129.

Public policies, change in, 90.

Public school system, development of, 161.

Reading, less time for, 74.

Recreation, forms of, 130.

Recreational education, 127, 129, 130.

Religion, paradox in, 86.

Research: objectives of, 7; co-operation in, 16.

Rousseau, theory of education of, 120.

Ruskin, John: on object of education, 42; quoted, 116, 122, 159.

Russell, Bertrand, quoted, 34, 121, 142.

Saturday Review of Literature, advertisement in, 105.

Scholarship, misconception of, 32.

School, definition of a, 125.

Science: in business and industry, 7; experiments with coal, oil and alcohol,

[176]

THE RELATIONS OF LEARNING, A Series of Addresses on University Education in a Changing World, By WILLIAM BENNETT BIZZELL, has been composed on the Monotype in twelve point Baskerville. John Baskerville began printing about 1750, after he had earlier amassed a fortune in the japanning trade. His first book, a quarto edition of Virgil, published seven years after he began his printing endeavors, was widely praised. A Latin Juvenal, finished in 1761, is perhaps his typographic masterpiece. Baskerville was constantly experimenting, not alone with type faces but with all branches of the printing art. He improved the standard of eighteenth century presswork, initiated a process of calendering paper and perfected a method of drying. His type, although based to some extent upon the work of his contemporary and competitor, Caslon, possesses more modern characteristics. Baskerville should properly be classed as a transitional face. There is more contrast between the heavy and thin lines, suggestive of modern Scotch Roman.

Baskerville has two pronounced identification points: the lower-case "g" has an unclosed loop; the capital and lower-case "j" have long flattened feet turned up with ball terminals. The Baskerville italic as cut for the Monotype is particularly satisfactory. It retains the most beautiful and unique features of the original —the ball terminals of the capital "T" and "N," and the grace stroke of the lower-case "p." Certain features of this book have been based upon the Latin Juvenal.

THE PRINTED PAGE IS EVERYMAN'S UNIVERSITY

UNIVERSITY OF OKLAHOMA PRESS
NORMAN